# CLARK THERAPY

# HEALTH AND PREVENTION
## FOR ALL AGES

Ignacio Chamorro Balda

1st Edition May 2013
© 2013 Ignacio Chamorro Balda
© of the edition in English: Dr. Clark Research Association
© of the edition in German: Dr. Clark Research Association
Design and cover: Mario Soria
Typographical and syntax correction: Maga Peña
Photographs: Valery Wallace.
ISBN: 84-000-0000-0
Legal deposit: B 000-2013
Printed by: i-loveprint.com
Printed in China

# DEDICATION

I would like to dedicate this book to several people who have accompanied me at all times:

*Dr. Clark, who taught me to learn*

*Dr. Fermín Moriano, who helped me to not give up*

*My father, Fernando Chamorro, from whom I learned what strength of will means*

*My grandparents, Drs. Ignacio Balda and Jesús Chamorro, I inherited my vocation from them*

*Thank you. I owe you everything I am professionally*

For more information on Dr. Hulda Clark visit www.drclark.net

# THANKS

First, I would like to give my most sincere thanks to my patients for trusting in me and in Clark Therapy.

To Luis Mateo, without whose help this book would not have been finished.

To José Antonio Campoy, for his honesty, courage and support to the health world.

To my mother, who gave me life.

And of course to Zara, who has accompanied me for so many years. I carry you in my heart.

I also thank CDC (Centers *for Disease Control and Prevention) and* DPDx *(Laboratory Identification of Parasites of Public Health Concern)* for allowing me the use of some of the photographs shown in this book.

I would also like to express my thanks to the authors that have given me images with which to illustrate this book:

Sherif Zaki and Wun-Ju Shieh, for the image of prions on page 26.

James Gathany, for the image of the mosquito *Anopheles* on page 33 and for the image of *Ascaris lumbricoides* on page 36.

9

What this book offers is not medical advice, but instead guidelines based on naturopathy, orthomolecular nutrition and bioresonance.

Please consult with your doctor to receive medical advice.
The recommendations set out herein do not necessarily imply that orthodox medicine agrees with them.

In writing this book, we have not based ourselves on clinical research or medical testing. Our results are based on examination and monitoring using the Syncrometer and the research done by Dr. Hulda Clark.

The objective of this work is to help the readers on their path to health.

In accordance with the results obtained by Dr. Hulda Clark, the Syncrometer is capable of detecting traces of toxins too small to be captured in a laboratory.

The Syncrometer does not offer quantitative results regarding the substances contained in the product. That can only be obtained in a laboratory.

Testing of people or saliva through which Clark Therapy has been developed does not constitute a medical diagnosis. It could be called "bioenergetic testing". This measuring system is not related to orthodox Western medicine and therefore, for the purposes of this medicine, it has no relevance or recognition.

# PROLOGUE BY DAVID P. AMREIN, ND

An incident in the summer of 1995 proved to be fateful for my future: I pulled a photocopied script out of one of my mother's cupboards, which turned out to be Dr. Hulda Clark's book "The Cure for All Cancers". A student in university back then, I was amazed at Dr. Clark's contentions about the cause of cancer and many other conditions and that it was possible to not only be healthy and stay healthy, but actually cure the most severe afflictions of mankind.

As incredible as Dr. Clark's claims were, they made me curious enough to travel to San Diego and visit her clinic, with the goal of talking to her patients and finding out whether the therapy was actually working and people were getting cured. To my own amazement, many of the patients at the clinic told me incredible stories of cures or improvements which orthodox medicine would have deemed impossible.

The basics of Dr. Hulda Clark's therapy were quite simple. Too simple, it seemed! And yet, they appeared to be workable. And even though there is a lot of information in Dr. Hulda Clark's books and even though she published a number of more technical books in the years that followed, the basics of her therapy have remained simple: remove the cause of an illness and the body will cure itself. And the causes of illnesses were generally toxins in our environment and parasites. And the treatments were simple enough that most people, unless they were very severely afflicted, could do something for their own health by themselves in their own homes. Like the Internet gave the power of information back to the people, Dr. Clark gave the power over our health back into our own hands!

And Dr. Clark's research was so comprehensive, so all-encompassing, that anyone can profit from her knowledge. Some of us to stay healthy, some of us to get healthy, and most of us to help a friend or acquaintance be healthy. Even pets can profit from Dr. Hulda Clark's protocol, being that she included pet health improvement programs in her books!

When I discovered Dr. Clark's work in 1995 and found out how much of a boon it is to mankind, I decided to dedicate my life to spreading this knowledge and helping as many people as I could. I

For more information on Dr. Hulda Clark visit www.drclark.net

started the first website about Dr. Clark and published many of her books in foreign languages to make them accessible to the world. Though it would have been easy for Dr. Clark to be satisfied with her work back in 1995, she kept working every day, 7 days a week, to do more research, come up with more explanations, with more treatment options, with faster, better and cheaper ways to cure. She worked almost until her final day and her last book came out posthumously – a book which, in many ways, was the culmination of her work.

Dr. Clark has left us 8 books, the result of 60 years of research and 46 years of medical practice. Now that Dr. Clark has passed, it is up to us to carry on her legacy. And I am very thankful that over the years, numerous well-intentioned and qualified therapists and researchers have come forward to contribute their research to Dr. Clark's – researchers in the US, in Italy, in Germany, in Switzerland, in Spain, in France and in other places, too numerous to enumerate.

One of these researchers is Ignacio Chamorro, whom I have been collaborating with since 2005. One of the most qualified therapists working with the Clark protocol, Ignacio Chamorro has also translated many of Dr. Clark's texts and books into Spanish, has trained hundreds of other therapists and prepared a whole Master course in Clark medicine. This immense amount of work was done to carry on Dr. Clark's legacy and bring it to the world, so that anyone can benefit from it.

This book that you are holding in your hands today is another important step to this end. Even though Dr. Clark's books are written for the layperson rather than the specialist, a sick person often wishes to inform themselves in little time to grasp the most important aspects of the therapy and get started. This book is therefore written from a very practical perspective, leaving out some of the more technical details which may not be of immediate interest.

It is my sincere hope that this book will allow even more people to discover Dr. Clark's work and use it to their benefit. Information is only valuable if it is known and used. I hope you find this book useful to familiarize yourself with the basic concepts of the Clark

For more information on Dr. Hulda Clark visit www.drclark.net

protocol and get started. If any questions remain, they are answered in Dr. Hulda Clark's books or at the seminars organized by Ignacio Chamorro or others, and we try to be accessible to anyone who has uncertainties and questions.

Sincerely,

**David P. Amrein**
Founder of
Dr. Clark Research Association

# PROLOGUE BY JOSÉ ANTONIO CAMPOY

In the past 15 years I have written or edited over two thousand news articles as well as over a thousand articles, interviews and reports, and have also read many more by very different authors, all on Health or Medicine. What's more, for professional reasons as well as for mere pleasure I have read in that same time no less than 150 books on very different topics and contents, leaving some half-read and leaving others after a few pages after having started them. And I have rejected writing prologues for several books whose authors did me the honor of asking for one, once I had read them, since it did not seem opportune to express my opinion, though I held their authors in esteem. I am incapable of speaking well - not even elegantly or diplomatically - of something I do not like; so I prefer not to. And I have the impression that Ignacio Chamorro, the author of this book, knew this very well when he asked me, which shows that he is firmly convinced that his book is interesting and that its contents are useful as well as reasonable. So, he is right: this book - literary qualities aside - is a compendium of useful and verified information as well as being pleasant and practical, so I am persuaded that it will be of interest to health professionals as well as to the public in general.

It could be argued that the author is not even a doctor - though his grandparents, paternal and maternal were - nor a biologist, chemist, pharmacist, and that the reader must therefore doubt what is said in the book, but they would be wrong because Ignacio Chamorro does not set out his own ideas or convictions - although he shares and completely adopts the contents - but instead those of the late Dr. Hulda R. Clark, a person with undeniable worldwide prestige, who exercised her profession for 46 years, along with an exhaustive research that was even longer - no less than 60 years - and ended up reflecting it in 8 books, the last of which would see the light after she passed on September 3, 2009, barely one month before she was to turn 81. She was born on October 18, 1928 in the old Soviet Union - in the heart of a Mennonite family - her parents emigrated to Canada when she was only 11 and she would complete most of her studies there. She held degrees in Physiology and Biology from the University of Saskatchewan (Canada) and in Biophysics and Cellular Physiology from the University of Minnesota (USA), and ended working as a naturopath in the United States where she worked for most of her life. Until she began to be hounded by the North American health authorities due to her affirmation that the origin of all so-called "illnesses" - including chronic illnesses, degenerative illnesses, autoimmune illnesses and cancer - is in environmental intoxication – including polluted air, bad quality water and the toxins in the food that we as well as animals ingest, nutritional deficits, the brutal current oxidizing

For more information on Dr. Hulda Clark visit www.drclark.net

stress on our bodies and the parasitic and microbial infections that are destroying this world, which made it necessary for her to move to Mexico, where she carried out her professional activities until the time of her death. In fact, when she died - despite her advanced age - she still directed the Century Nutrition Clinic in Tijuana. A death that would not prevent her from being slandered and vilified unjustly and without foundation by those who for years attempted to silence or ridicule her magnificent work. Regarding the knowledge that she acquired, she set it forth in eight books published in English, many of which were translated into Spanish, German, Italian, Russian and numerous other languages: The Cure for All Cancers, the Cure for All Advanced Cancers, The Prevention of All Cancers, The Cure and Prevention of All Cancers, The Cure for HIV and AIDS, Syncrometer Science Laboratory Manual and The Cure for All Diseases.

I must add that the undersigned had the honor and pleasure to know her personally since her presentation closed the Second International Congress on Complementary and Alternative Treatments of Cancer which under the sponsorship of the World Association for Cancer Research (WACR) - that I am honored to preside over - and with the support of Discovery DSALUD (www.dsalud.com) - a publication that I have the pleasure to direct - was held at the Palace of Congresses and Exhibitions of Madrid on May 26 and 27, 2007. She attended this Congress, coming from Mexico, at age 78, thanks to the intervention of Ignacio Chamorro, for whom I know she had a deep affection.

The author of this book knew Dr. Hulda Clark very well on a personal as well as on a professional level. He made good use of a long time spent with her at her clinic in Tijuana and has also translated some of her work into Spanish. This in my opinion is sufficient to know that the book that I have been honored to ask to prologue is faithful to her ideas and postulates. Because this book is that above all: an attempt - complex and difficult obviously - to summarize in a few pages the essential part of her discoveries, something that given the volume of work published by Dr. Clark must not have been easy. And I sincerely believe that he has done this successfully. Because instead of justifying each of the doctor's affirmations, he has chosen to summarize them and accept them, knowing that whoever is interested in going into more depth on each aspect has the 8 books that she published at his disposal (actually she wrote 9 but the first was not related to health). He has written, in short, a book that is characterized by pragmatism. He explains the fundamentals of the basics on which what Hulda Clark postulated is grounded, but above all, he summarizes in a lucid manner how any person can face not only a minor health problem but also a serious chronic type of problem, auto-immune or degenerative problem, including cancer. It will be said that such a thing is not possible because each pathology requires a specific treatment protocol, but such an affirmation is no more than a fallacy assumed uncritically by the immense majority of doctors who since they were students in the faculties of medicine have had a large amount of information hidden from them while they were mentally programmed to accept without reservations the "gospel truths" established and transmitted first by their "teachers" at university and then by the "leaders" of medical opinion when they had obtained their degrees; and since then they ask themselves, terrified, what to do when faced with a real patient because the immense majority leave university incapable of diagnosing 99% of the so-called "illnesses" that they have been told exist - today tens of thousands - and much less how to treat them since they have been assured that the majority are of "idiopathic etiology" - in plain terms: of unknown cause -although they then suggest "possible risk factors" to be treated with pharmaceuticals that are merely palliative. The reality is that the so-called illnesses do not exist and that all pathologies that human beings suffer from have the same causes already described, so the treatment must always be the same: deep detoxification, controlling what we breathe, drink and ingest, eliminating foods to which we are allergic or intolerant, learning to prepare them without overheating them, frying them or putting them in the microwave, avoiding all processed or canned foods as well as those that contain synthetic additives (preservatives, dyes, aromas or artificial sweeteners), drinking only pure water from low mineralization springs - or, better yet, distilled water - not ingesting transgenics, discarding the consumption of iatrogenic pharmaceuticals, not using damaging synthetic clothing, not smoking or taking drugs, avoiding artificial and telluric electromagnetic radiation, sunbathing, exercising, resting sufficiently, facing psycho-emotional problems intelligently, eliminating from the body all possible parasites or pathogenic microbes and when applicable, supplementing the diet orthomolecularly. Dr. Clark proposed concrete protocols to face the most complex questions, which she reached after several decades of study and research and which Ignacio Chamorro sets out simply in this book for the knowledge of the public in general and not only health professionals. Knowledge that is summarized in following some simple steps:

1. Preferably drink distilled water and even cook with it.
2. Breathe unpolluted air.
3. Do moderate exercise daily.
4. Ingest only ecological products and not transgenic ones, free from pesticides, herbicides, fungicides, insecticides, chemical fertilizers and synthetic additives.
5. Do not use clothes or hygiene products that contain synthetic chemical substances.
6. Do not consume fried, pre-cooked, canned or microwave-heated food.
7. Do not consume drugs, including tobacco, alcohol and synthetic iatrogenic pharmaceuticals that flood our society.
8. Eliminate all possible amalgams from the teeth (ensuring that this is done properly).
9. Avoid electromagnetic contamination.
10. Ensure that you sunbathe daily - at suitable hours - and when this is not possible, use a total spectrum light lamp.
11. Stimulate the immune system and nourish the body appropriately, when necessary with orthomolecular supplements.
12. Detoxify the body by deep cleansing the intestines, kidneys and liver with the protocols and devices developed by Dr. Clark herself to get rid of possible parasites, pathogenic microbes and toxins (including heavy metals).

This is an efficacious program in which it is often useful to be helped by some of the devices designed by Dr. Clark and which Ignacio Chamorro describes in his book, explaining simply how to use them. I refer to the water distiller, the VariZapper, the Zappicator, the Ozonator, the Colloidal Silver Maker and the so-called Full Spectrum Light Box. And, of course, to the products tested and proposed by Dr. Clark that help on one hand to detoxify the body and on the other hand, to nourish it suitably, balance it energetically and biochemically, and to stimulate the immune system. I end these lines by saying that I have sufficient information to know that what Dr. Hulda Clark postulated - without going into any nuances that do not alter the substance of this affirmation - is correct and borne out by the results obtained from thousands of patients that followed her suggestions. This is why I do not hesitate to congratulate Ignacio Chamorro for his excellent summarizing work.

**José Antonio Campoy**
DSALUD Discovery Director
President of the World Association for Cancer Research (WACR)

# INTRODUCTION

I began my professional work in the world of health several years ago, initially dedicating myself exclusively to nutrition and supplements for elite athletes. This sector taught me many things that are not taken into account by sports professionals and much less by the rest of the population, among them something as fundamental as seeking the prevention of health imbalances, called injuries, illnesses, physical overloads, psychic overloads, etc., before they happen.

*Ignacio Chamorro with Dr. Clark in 2008*

We all have the idea in our heads that when something in our body or mind fails, the solution is to go to the doctor for a cure, without further analysis most of the times that this happens, leaving it always in the hands of the "health professionals", without asking ourselves the reason for that imbalance and the manner in which to prevent it. We have been taught to think that it is normal for us to get ill, to be injured, that our blood pressure and sugar rises at a certain age, that arthrosis and osteoporosis are part of our lives, that we can do little to ease the effects of illness or slow them down, that we must take medication which is often toxic (and in most cases has repercussions on our health, causing serious damage)... We have been taught to think that it is normal when it is not.

In the field of sports, I saw with much sadness often how some athletes ended their professional careers due to repeated injuries, which in many cases arose from severe nutritional deficits maintained for a long time, or from undetected chronic infections that involved a drop in performance, problems with metabolism, etc., due to not having following some basic guidelines that should have been given by the people who were in charge of their care. And all of this due to lack of knowledge.

Another of the countless examples of this lack of knowledge can be seen by being aware that most of the population has never heard of heavy metals, and up to a certain point this may be normal; what is not normal is the number of people in charge of our health that do not know anything about their toxicity and the problems that they can cause us directly or indirectly. It has been studied, it has been published and it is on the internet, so why are they not interested? I sincerely think that it is because the term "prevention" is not yet on the hard drive of many of these healthcare professionals, since they have been taught to prescribe and not to prevent.

21

It is very normal for us to be prescribed medication filled with aluminum and othe toxins only for prevention, regardless of the possible side effects that are alread known. Apart from all of that, what I am trying to highlight in this book is that w should prevent and treat by looking for the origin of the problem and not ae against the symptoms. How many people do we know with chronic anemia, whic are only recommended to take iron, without looking at the possible causes of th anemia (parasitosis, metal intoxication, excess oxidants, etc.)? Probably many. Th happens with our health, and must change. We must begin to know how to prever disease and, of course, how to improve our quality of life. And what is mo important: we ourselves must begin to take charge of our health and bas prevention, following a series of very effective basic principles. But we must als know how to do this without attacking our bodies with pharmaceuticals that most have more side effects than possible benefits.

In this book I try to show the reader some health principles created by my dear missed Dr. Clark, principles that try to eliminate the causes of practically all healt problems, which are two: toxins and pathogens.

Believe me, these two factors are the causative factors of most illnesses and in man cases of drops in physical or mental performance, whether you are a normal perso or an elite athlete.

We must all take some nutritional supplements if we hope to live better and longe Possibly a couple of decades ago it was not as necessary as it is now, because mayb our grandparents were not as exposed as we are to toxins in our entir surroundings: water, food, air, hygiene products, etc.

This is the fundamental reason why we need to help our bodies to eliminate th toxins as well as the pathogens through a specific supplementation to detoxify th liver, kidney, intestines, etc.

Of course years ago there were parasites just as there are now, but since peop were not as intoxicated, they could defend themselves with their immune system not so now. We must simply look around us to see the "epidemic" of degenerativ mental, auto-immune pathologies, etc., and analyze the results of orthodo treatments. In this book I want you to receive a basis to be able to help you and he your loved ones to prevent disease and improve your health because I believe th INFORMATION ON HEALTH AND PREVENTION IS A RIGHT OF EVERY HUMA BEING, although certain vested interests are more interested in us continuing to k ignorant in this matter. I offer you a very small but very valuable part of the resear of a great scientist named Hulda R. Clark.

I sincerely hope that this book is of help to you.

Ignacio Chamor Madrid, May 6, 201

# INDEX

| | | |
|---|---|---|
| 1 | What is Clark Therapy? | 27 |
| 2 | What is a parasite? | 29 |
| 3 | Different types of pathogens | 31 |
| 4 | First cause of illness: pathogens | 33 |
| 5 | The problem of diagnosis | 37 |
| 6 | Types of parasites | 38 |
| 7 | Some examples of parasites | 41 |
| 8 | How to deparasitize ourselves | 48 |
| 9 | The digestive system, the basis of our health | 51 |
| 10 | The Clark Program of intestinal cleansing + Oregano oil | 62 |
| 11 | Properties of the supplements used in the intestinal cleansing program | 64 |
| 12 | Classic Parasite Program for adults | 69 |
| 13 | Classic Parasite Program for children | 71 |
| 14 | Classic Parasite Program for pets | 72 |
| 15 | Properties of the supplements used in the classic Parasite Program | 74 |
| 16 | Ascaris Parasite Program | 75 |
| 17 | Properties of the supplements used in the Ascaris Parasite Program | 76 |
| 18 | Possible detoxification symptoms after parasite cleansing | 78 |
| 19 | Eliminating pathogens from foods | 79 |
| 20 | The true protagonists of our illnesses | 80 |

| 21 | Auto-immune conditions | 82 |
| 22 | The pathways used by parasites to enter and exit | 86 |
| 23 | How is the presence of parasites diagnosed in the body? | 88 |
| 24 | Why do we get ill more often nowadays? Clark Therapy and improving the immune system | 90 |
| 25 | What is a toxin? | 91 |
| 26 | Main sources of toxins | 92 |
| 27 | Stimulating our immune systems | 96 |
| 28 | The five basic immunosuppressants | 98 |
| 29 | Why are heavy metals so dangerous? | 101 |
| 30 | How can heavy metals be avoided? | 103 |
| 31 | The problem with water | 105 |
| 32 | How to support our immune system | 108 |
| 33 | Eliminating toxins: the detoxification organs and the organ cleanses | 111 |
| 34 | Kidney Cleansing | 112 |
| 35 | Kidney Cleansing protocol + Oregano oil | 114 |
| 36 | Properties of the supplements used in the Kidney Cleanse | 116 |
| 37 | Liver cleansing | 117 |
| 38 | Why cleanse the liver? | 119 |
| 39 | Controversies over liver cleansing | 122 |
| 40 | Liver cleansing protocol | 124 |
| 41 | Elimination of toxins | 126 |
| 42 | Detoxification program for heavy metals and other toxins | 127 |

For more information on Dr. Hulda Clark visit www.drclark.net

| 43 | Dr. Clark's health protocol | 130 |
| 44 | Why do we follow these steps? | 131 |
| 45 | Another enemy of our health: oxidative stress | 132 |
| 46 | Clark Therapy Antioxidant cocktail | 136 |
| 47 | Specialized equipment used in Clark Therapy – VariZapper | 139 |
| 48 | Specialized equipment used in Clark Therapy – Zapplates | 147 |
| 49 | specialized equipment used in Clark Therapy – Food Zappicator | 153 |
| 50 | Specialized equipment used in Clark Therapy – Ozonator | 156 |
| 51 | Specialized equipment used in Clark Therapy – Water distiller | 163 |
| 52 | Specialized equipment used in Clark Therapy – Colloidal Silver Maker | 166 |
| 53 | Specialized equipment used in Clark Therapy – Full Spectrum Light Box | 172 |
| 54 | Frequently asked questions by patients about Clark Therapy | 179 |
| 55 | Guide of products used in Clark Therapy | 190 |
| 56 | Directory of Clark Therapists | 232 |
| 57 | Holistic Dentists | 239 |
| 58 | Authorized distributors of Clark products | 243 |

For more information on Dr. Hulda Clark visit www.drclark.net

# WHAT IS CLARK THERAPY?

Clark Therapy is a self-health system created by Dr. Hulda R. Clark, a Canadian researcher, who discovered that the origin of 95% of illnesses derives from the presence of parasites and toxins in the body.

What do we mean by a self-health system? Well, when these pathogens and toxins are eliminated, the body recovers its normal functions by itself, that is, we do not force it in any way to modify its natural functions. By simply cleansing our body from these two elements that are foreign to it, it will begin to recover its functions and health.

The main characteristic of Clark Therapy is that we treat the body as a whole, understanding that our organs are interrelated, so if one of them is overloaded or contains parasites, this will not only affect it, but will directly or indirectly have an effect on the functioning of other organs and therefore on our entire body. This view is contrary to other types of medicine, in which there is a specialist for each bodily organ or system, who is only concerned with the organs that are in their specialty, believing that the health of the sick organ or system will depend on a specific treatment, without understanding that probably the origin of this pathology or symptomatology can be found in another organ or system.

Our body is an interrelated and complete system and we have to treat it as such. We must understand for example that a skin condition is probably the reflection of having parasites or an excess of toxins in the liver, or that depression could possibly derive from excessive intestinal waste. This is the reason for which in most cases, treatments recommended by certain health professionals often only attenuate some symptoms and rarely end the disease, since they do not attack its origin, but instead focus exclusively on the "tip of the iceberg".

In Clark Therapy on the other hand, we understand that medicine that could be damaging or toxic to our bodies should never be used. We simply use medicine from the orthomolecular or herbal realm, such as vitamins, minerals, herbal extracts, etc.

In the past few years, Clark Therapy has benefited hundreds of thousands of people worldwide, treating innumerable health problems: diabetes, hepatitis, irritable bowel syndrome, Crohn's disease, depression, cancer, AIDS, pains of all types, arthritis, dermatitis, psoriasis and so on. With a very high percentage of recovery and complete solutions to the problem, and most importantly, WITHOUT HEALTH RISKS

For more information on Dr. Hulda Clark visit www.drclark.net

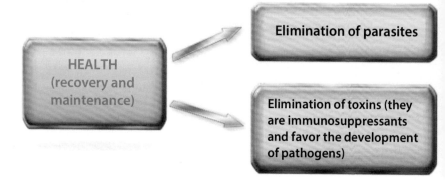

With these two principles we can stop or slow the evolution of practically all illnesses, and completely eliminate a high percentage of them.

# WHAT IS A PARASITE?

It is an organism that penetrates our body seeking shelter and food, and once housed in it, begins to multiply to ensure its survival. Parasites can cause us damage directly or indirectly: in addition to altering our functions, damaging our tissues and stealing our nutrients, they can intoxicate us with products derived from their metabolism.

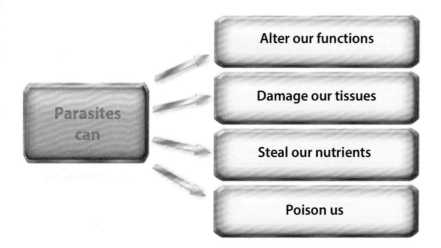

And although other branches of medicine do not concern themselves much with parasites, we must know that they will ALWAYS harm us.

In Clark Therapy, practically all illnesses have their origin in parasites. But we must also mention that there are other types of pathogens that are also implicated in many diseases, being directly responsible for the illness, or collaborating in the deterioration of our functions along with other pathogens. This means that only rarely do we find only one family of pathogens in a specific illness, and even though the patient has been diagnosed with a virus, bacterium, protozoon, fungus or parasite, there are always several different families of pathogens working closely together. This is what Dr. Clark termed "pathogen gangs". Notwithstanding this, we always give the protagonist role in our disorders to parasites, because they are the origin of the disorders, because they cause the damage directly or because inside they carry bacteria, viruses, protozoa and fungi.

Isn't it curious? We can now finally understand why these bacterial infection do not abate after long months of treatment with antibiotics, cases candidiasis recur for years, and specific localized infections relapse. The reaso is simply that the pathogen that appeared at a specific moment was attacke without understanding that its carrier also had to be treated, that is, one several families of parasites.

This fact was discovered by Dr. Clark when she began to experiment with th Zapper (a device she created, which we will discuss later) in order to eliminat parasites from the body, realizing that when these die off, other pathoger that had not previously been detected in testing, mainly bacteria and fung emerge from inside them. Also, when the zapping eliminated bacteria, viruse which had not previously been detected appeared from their "cadavers".

> **The parasites tend to be carriers of bacteria, viruses, protozoa and fungi**

For more information on Dr. Hulda Clark visit www.drclark.net

# DIFFERENT TYPES OF PATHOGENS

et's list them briefly:

**PARASITES:** They are multi-celled beings that take their nourishment from the fluids of the host. Often they feed by sucking its blood, although some feed on bile, such as *Clonorchis sinensis,* or even devour the tissue, creating tunnels and erosions.

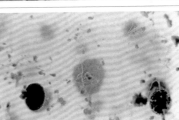

**PROTOZOA:** They are single-celled organisms that are almost always microscopic, although they are eukaryotes, which gives them a cell structure more similar to animals and plants than bacteria. (Eukaryote cellular organisms are those that have a differentiated nucleus, where their genetic information is concentrated, and this nucleus is protected by a membrane.)

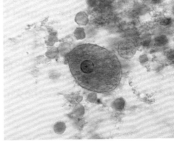

**BACTERIA:** They are single-celled beings, with their genetic material not concentrated in a cellular membrane, that is, they are prokaryotes and the majority are microscopic.

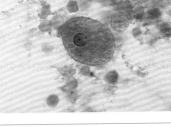

**FUNGI:** They are further classified into mold and yeast. These micro-organisms proliferate when our immune system is low or when taking antibiotics destroys the intestinal flora, which is then replaced by fungi and pathogenic bacteria.

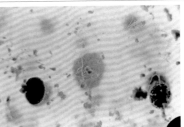

> **But undoubtedly, for those of us who practice Clark Therapy, the most important pathogens and therefore the first ones that we must deal with in order to solve any type of health problem, are parasites, for several reasons:**

- They are causative factors of all degenerative conditions.
- They are carriers of bacteria, fungi and viruses that in turn generate diverse health problems.
- They themselves can generate illnesses directly.

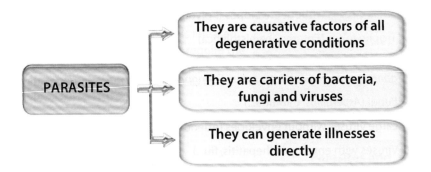

We can find parasites directly responsible for diseases – a relationship which is, in most cases, not accepted by orthodox medicine – such as for example:

- **Migraines**: *Strongyloides* tend to be found.

- **Addictions:** we also tend to find colonies of *Strongyloides* in the brain's center of addiction.

- **Chronic fatigue syndrome:** linked to the parasite *Cryptostrongylus* pulmoni

- **Cancer:** almost fifty pathogens are implicated – though maybe the most important of these are Fasciolopsis buski and Ascaris lumbricoides.

- **Mutations** giving rise to Down syndrome, cystic fibrosis or polycystic kidneys, linked to the Gastrothylax parasite.

For more information on Dr. Hulda Clark visit www.drclark.net

- **Neurological illnesses** such as neurocysticercosis, linked to Cysticercus, which is a larval form of the tapeworm Taenia solium.

- **Bruxism:** due to parasites in the nervous system or nerve irritation caused by parasitic toxins released in the digestive tract.

- **Appendicitis:** linked in all cases to Oxyuris.

- **Depression:** linked to Ancylostomas, Strongyloides and Trichinella.

- **Schizophrenia:** linked to Ancylostoma braziliense, Ancylostoma caninum, Strongyloides, Ascaris, Shigella and Mycobacterium phlei.

- **Epilepsy:** Ascaris or Ancylostoma larvae block the production of GABA

- **Renal failures:** it is normal to find Fasciolopis buski, tapeworms, Echinoporyphium recurvatum and Ancylostomas.

- **Diabetes:** almost always Eurytrema pancreaticum is directly responsible.

- **Destruction of organs:** The majority of parasites can damage tissue.

- **Multiple chemical sensitivity:** linked in all cases to Fasciola hepatica

Also, any of the parasites of the trematode group (Fasciolopsis buski, Eurytrema pancreaticum and Clonorchis sinensis) can produce the following ailments:

- **Muscular dystrophy**

- **Cramps and bleeding** outside the menstrual period or endometriosis if they go through the intestinal wall.

- **Diabetes**

- **Alzheimer's and multiple** sclerosis if they complete their cycle in the brain.

- **Immunodepression** if they invade the thymus.

For more information on Dr. Hulda Clark visit www.drclark.net

Other types of pathogens are also directly related in other pathologies: Recently, Alzheimer's disease has been associated with the Herpes virus. In fact, Herpes viral encephalitis affects the same brain centers that are damaged in cases of Alzheimer's.

Also, in the past few years, it has been discovered that one of every three cases of obesity may be caused by infection with Adenovirus 36 and pathogens such *as Chlamydia pneumoniae, Porphyromonas gingivalis, Helicobacter pylori, Influenzavirus A*, hepatitis C virus and Cytomegalovirus contribute to forming atheroma plaques.
Parkinson's has also been related to the bacteria *Nocardia asteroides*.

**Apart from the damage that they can cause from their own activity, many parasites can poison us with products from their metabolism. Some examples of this are the following toxins:**

- **Forbol:** stimulates the growth of tumors produced by *Fasciolopsis buski* larvae.

- **Beta-propiolactone:** powerful mutagen produced by *Ascaris*.

- **Ortho-phospho-tyrosine**: mainly responsible for tumors becoming malign, produced by *the Fasciolopsis buski* larvae.

- **1,10-phenanthroline:** oxidizes our vitamin C and forms large unusable quantities of iron compounds in the body. It is also produced by *Ascaris*.

- **20-methylcholanthrene:** is the greatest carcinogen known, it is also produced by *Ascaris*.

# THE PROBLEM OF DIAGNOSIS

D r. Clark was convinced that the main problem of orthodox medicine lies in the diagnosis, that is, in its incapacity to know the real cause that provokes an ailment, simply because its current methods only allow knowing the current condition of an organ or of a system, but not what has led the person to that situation – and because doctors hardly ever look for possible parasitosis or toxins in the body because they have not been taught to.

Some reasons for which the diagnosis of parasites is difficult for allopathic medicine are the following:

- A parasite is like a leech. The adult attaches to a point inside our body where it produces thousands of eggs. Its attachment causes small chronic bleeding which ends up causing anemia and pain. We are not capable of expelling them alive or dead because they are stuck to our tissues, they are not circulating through the blood, so they are more difficult to detect.

- Parasites (in their adult as well as larva phase) are too soft and small to appear on a scanner. With the Syncrometer (device created by Dr. Clark) we can locate them, because we detect the frequencies that they emit inside the human body, and we can also see what organ(s) they have colonized.

- Biopsies that use orthodox medicine are prepared by cutting the tissue in very fine sheets. No sheet of a parasite would be recognizable. A biologist can find them, but only if he knows where to look.

- Parasites protect themselves with mucopolysaccharides (components of our connective tissue) that the immune system does not detect. For example: *Trypanosoma cruzi* acquires antigens from neurons, Schistosoma from the A, B and O blood groups, and *Onchocerca* from the retina. Many parasites, throughout their lives, change the type of mucopolysaccharide with which they protect themselves, depending on the organ they colonize, for example, *Plasmodium*, Toxoplasma, Taenia, *Dirofilaria*...

- Parasites tend to settle in organs with less immunological activity like the brain, female and male reproductive system, and organs with more toxins.

- All parasites can colonize any organ (to the contrary of what orthodox medicine believes).

- They inhibit the proper functioning of the immune system.

For more information on Dr. Hulda Clark visit www.drclark.net

# TYPES OF PARASITES

**We can classify them into two main groups:**

1. **HELMINTHS:** they can measure from fractions of an inch to many feet in length and are invertebrates. They are divided into two types:

■ <u>Plathelminthes</u> (flat). They are hermaphrodites. They are divided into several types:

a) Cestodes: they are segmented. They do not have a digestive tract, so they feed through their skin. They are divided by segments: the first segment is named "scolex" and is characterized by having anchoring structures. The rest of the segments are named "proglottids".

Some examples are: *Taenia solium, Taenia saginata, Hymenolepsis, and Diphyllobothrium latum*.

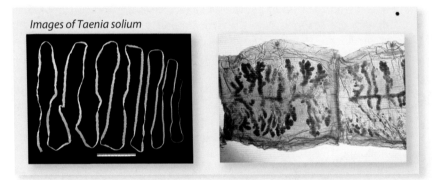

Images of Taenia solium

b) <u>Trematodes:</u> they are not segmented. They have a digestive tract, although rudimentary, and two suckers with which they anchor themselves and feed.

Some examples are: Fasciola hepatica, *Fasciolopsis buski* and *Schistosomas*.

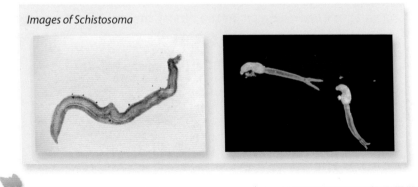

Images of Schistosoma

For more information on Dr. Hulda Clark visit <u>www.drclark.net</u>

- Nematodes (round): Their digestive system is more developed, they have a nervous system and their sexes are differentiated.

  Some examples are: *Ascaris lumbricoides, Ascaris megalocephala, Enterobius vermicularis, Ancylostoma, Dirofilaria, Strongyloides, Toxocara, Necator americanus, Trichinella spiralis* and *Trichuris trichiura.*

*Images of Strongyloides*

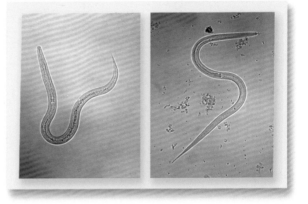

2. **ARTHROPODS:** they are invertebrates, have an exterior skeleton and developed legs, their sexes are differentiated and they can be of different sizes. Some examples are: flies, mosquitoes, ticks, fleas, lice and mites.

They are also transmitters of other parasites, bacteria and viruses, for example:

- Fleas transmit: typhus, plague, Taenia and Lyme Disease
- Ticks transmit: Q fever, Rickettsiosis, encephalitis and also Lyme Disease
- Flies and mosquitoes transmit: malaria, dengue fever, encephalitis, yellow fever, *Trypanosoma, Leishmania, Dirofilaria,* and *Onchocerca.*

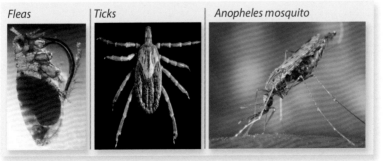

| Fleas | Ticks | Anopheles mosquito |

39

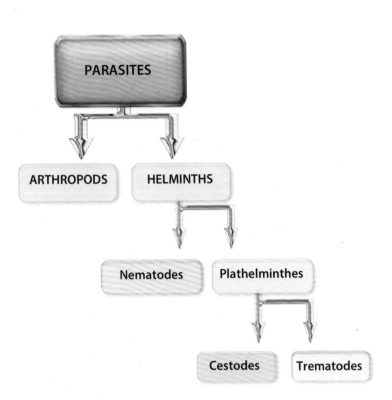

# SOME EXAMPLES OF PARASITES

After having listed the different types or families of parasites, in this section we will go into more depth on specific families of parasites which are maybe the most important ones in Clark Therapy, not only because they are found in a very high percentage of the population, but also because each one of them can have certain interesting particularities, which are worthy of listing:

## 1. *Ascaris lumbricoides*

A quarter of the world population is infected with the parasite Ascaris lumbricoides. In general, the infecting egg reaches our small intestine, where it releases the larva that subsequently can go through the intestinal wall to reach the portal circulation (to the liver) through the blood vessels that nourish the

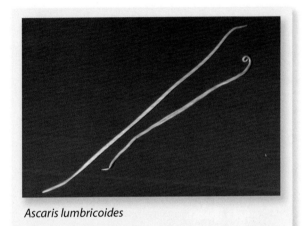

*Ascaris lumbricoides*

small intestine. From here it reaches the liver and from there can reach any organ when the larvae-infested blood leaves through the liver veins into the general circulation. Then the Ascaris larvae reach the heart and then the lungs, from which they can reach the alveoli, the bronchioles and the bronchia. From here it is possible that they go up the throat and thus reach the esophagus, stomach, pancreas, kidneys, appendix, uterus, prostate, hearing channels, and even the brain and the tear ducts.

Ascaris damages the tissue of the small intestine and of the organs that it colonizes. It also produces inflammatory phenomena in the tissue that it infects. When it reaches the respiratory system it causes an excess of mucus. It can also produce the so-called eosinophilic pneumonia, asthma, bronchitis, bronchiolitis, nasopharynx obstructions and inflammations, intestinal occlusions, appendicitis, pancreatitis, liver abscesses, allergies, alterations in protein digestion, and rob us of our nutrients.

41

Orthodox medicine's diagnosis is done by looking for the presence of eggs in the fecal material, which in our opinion is not very reliable, since an Ascaris female can lay eggs in any organ, not only in the small intestine, as affirmed by orthodox medicine.

Allopathic medicine also has immunological tests, based on the detection of antibodies, to establish indirect diagnoses. But these are not very reliable since the test may cross-react with *Strongyloides, Dirofilaria, Toxocara canis, Trichinella spiralis* and others.

*Ascaris lumbricoides*

Another diagnosis used by medicine is the molecular method, with which nucleic acids of different parasites are detected. In our opinion, they do not always detect the presence of parasites.

The pharmaceuticals used against Ascaris are toxic and can produce liver alterations and intestinal irritations.

The action mechanism of these parasite purging agents used in orthodox medicine generally produces the immobilization of the parasite, so it cannot attach to the intestinal wall and is excreted, but this does not always involve its death. In our opinion, this method may be valid only when the parasites are found at the intestinal level, but not so when they are found in other organs. And it is their presence in these other organs that can cause us serious health problems.

We must highlight the following regarding *Ascaris*:

- They can migrate to any organ.

- Females lay approximately 200,000 eggs daily in the intestine, which makes us see the importance of eradicating not only adult parasites and larvae, but also their eggs, which is impossible with pharmaceutical medication.

- They can produce: asthma, bronchitis, bronchiolitis, eczema, psoriasis, mumps, Herpes, night sweats and epileptic seizures.

- They are carriers of the Papillomavirus and of the Adenovirus (common cold).

- They contribute to cancer in several ways:
    - They generate chromosomal ruptures.
    - They create tricalcium phosphate deposits, which cover and protect numerous types of cancer.
    - They block the telomerase inhibitor, promoting the development of the tumor.
    - They block cathepsin B, which is a defensive enzyme against tumor cells.
    - -They are carriers of the NEU oncovirus.

## 2. Pinworm (*Enterobius vermicularis*)

- Is usually found in the rectum.
- Females cause anal irritation during the night.
- They can cause:

    - Menstrual pain, being present in most of these cases.

    - Night agitation and insomnia in children and adults (since most of the parasite's activity is at night).

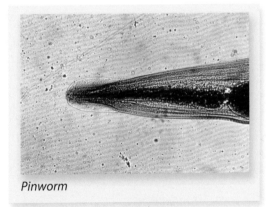

Pinworm

    - Intestinal problems because they irritate the intestine walls that they move along; they tend to generate microtrauma in the mucosa, in which a bacterial colonization is subsequently produced.

    - Urogenital infections. In the case of women, they can cause damage to the bladder, vagina, fallopian tubes and cervix. And in men they can generate inflammation in the prostate, bladder and penis.

    - Many cases of appendicitis

For more information on Dr. Hulda Clark visit www.drclark.net

### 3. *Ancylostoma*

- Present in most cases of ulcerative colitis.

- They can cause:

    - Epileptic attacks and coma.
    - Bronchitis.
    - Lymphatic inflammations.
    - Anemia.
    - Cysts.
    - Duodenitis.
    - Diarrhea.
    - Anemia.
    - Renal insufficiency and other problems in the kidneys.

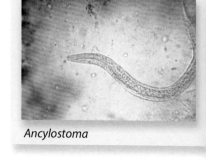

*Ancylostoma*

- It is important to highlight that they can affect us transcutaneously: the larva pass through the skin of unprotected feet or hands, reaching the blood flow and from there the heart, lungs, intestines, kidneys, brain...

- They can survive for six years within us.

*Ancylostoma*

### 4. *Strongyloides*

Although their habitat is the small intestine, they can migrate to any organ, such as the lungs, brain, kidneys, liver, bile ducts, pancreas, ganglia, heart and skeletal muscles.

- They cause hypothalamic erosion, which is the first step in all cancers.

- They carry:

    - Fungi
    - SRC oncovirus.
    - Cytomegalovirus.

*Strongyloides*

For more information on Dr. Hulda Clark visit www.drclark.net

- Epstein-Barr Virus (EBV).
- Bacteria that cause meningitis, abscesses, etc.
- Contagion may be through the skin (as with Ancylostoma).
- In recent years, a notable increase of infections with this parasite has occurred in patients treated with immunomodulators.

### 5. *Clonorchis sinensis*

The infection may occur by consuming freshwater fish raw, dry, in brine, or in marinade, whose meat contains encysted larvae. It is recommended that these fish be frozen for at least 24 hours before eating them, although the larvae can also be found in other plant food such as watercress, lettuce, alfalfa, etc.

- Causes erosions in the pituitary gland that are the second step of all cancers.
- Brings the hepatitis B virus.
- Can produce bile duct obstruction, hepatitis and pancreatitis

*Clonorchis sinensis*

### 6. *Eurytrema pancreaticum*

- Present in all cases of diabetes (type I or type II diabetes).
- Causes erosions in the pancreas that will contribute to the formation of tumor nuclei in any organ.
- Carries SV40 oncovirus.
- We can be infected by consuming meat of any mammal and vegetables that may have been in contact with ground snails, which tend to be carriers of their eggs.

*Eurytrema pancreaticum*

45

## 7. *Fasciolopsis buski*

- Forms OPT (ortho-phospho-tyrosine), which causes tumors to become malignant.
- The cercaria (non-adult) stage produces hGC (human chorionic gonadotropin), the main defender of tumors.
- When they die they release Salmonellas.
- They carry the MYC oncovirus.
- They carry the flu virus.
- They block cathepsin B.
- Carrier of the Bacillus cereus bacterium, which in turn causes allergies in all the organs with parasites and converts a multitude of hormones into an invalid form.
- It is a carrier of Candida and converts into the best protector of those fungi when there is an excessive population of Fasciolopsis.
- It tends to invade us orally through food of the same type as the Eurytrema pancreaticum.
- The adult parasite can survive for up to one year in the human body.

*Fasciolopsis buski*

## 8. *Onchocerca*

- Forms abdominal masses (lymphomas).
- Carrier of CEA (carcinoembryonic antigen)
- Blocks various enzymes in cancer patients:
    - Ubiquitin.
    - Cathepsin B.
    - Telomerase inhibitor.
- It brings the JUN oncovirus.
- It is present in the majority of cases of varicose veins since it places itself in the vein valves, impeding them from closing correctly.
- The infection can be orally or through flies and mosquitoes.
- The adult parasite can survive up to 15 years in the human body.

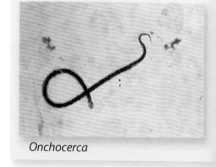

*Onchocerca*

### 9. *Fasciola* hepatica

- The infection can be transmitted orally.
- It forms abdominal masses (lymphomas).
- It can produce hepatitis, intestinal inflammations, pancreatitis, hives and stenosis of the bile ducts.
- It can survive for over ten years in our bile ducts.

*Fasciola hepatica*

### 10. *Dirofilaria*

- Forms abnormal abdominal masses
- Forms Hodgkin's lymphomas.
- Brings FOS oncovirus.
- Brings Mycobacterium phlei.
- Causes heart attacks in most cases in which its development is not stopped.
- It is curiously named the "dog heart parasite", when it infects more humans than dogs.

*Dirofilaria immitis*

# HOW TO DEPARASITE OURSELVES

There are several protocols used in Clark Therapy to deparasitize ourselves as well as our children and pets.

We can divide the Parasite Programs into:

A. On one side, the so-called **Bowel Cleanse (indispensable)** and the **classic Parasite Program (which is not strictly necessary if the Bowel Cleanse has been done, although it is recommended),** which cover the majority of parasites due to the wide spectrum of the fundamental ingredient in the two protocols, which is black walnut hull tincture.

B. On the other side, the protocol named ***Ascaris* Parasite Program** (it is fundamental because these parasites, as well as the rest of the nematodes, are only eliminated with this protocol), which eliminates these parasites and the other families that are not sensitive to black walnut hull tincture, such as the *Ancylostomas*, tapeworms, pinworms, *Strongyloides*, *Trichinellas*, *Trichuris*, etc. That is, practically all nematodes and cestodes.

It is always a good idea to carry out the Bowel Cleanse (followed if you wish by the classic Parasite Program) and subsequently the *Ascaris* Parasite Program because we habitually carry different types of parasites and doing only one type of Parasite Program is not sufficient, since we would not kill them all.

C. **Electronically with the Zapper** frequency generator invented by Dr. Hulda Clark that eliminates pathogens from our bodies, and in turn stimulates the immune system (there is more complete information on the VariZapper in the chapter dedicated to specialized equipment).

In parallel to the use of the VariZapper, it is **indispensable** that the Parasite Programs with herbs and supplements be carried out (Bowel Cleanse and *Ascaris* Parasite Program), since the effect of the VariZapper does not reach inside the intestines or organs that are very burdened with solvents. It is always important to continue with kidney and liver cleansings in parallel to the use of the VariZapper, once the Bowel Cleanse and the *Ascaris* Parasite Program have been carried out.

For more information on Dr. Hulda Clark visit www.drclark.net

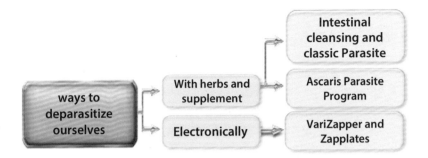

**Why do we do the Bowel Cleanse first instead of the classic Parasite Program?**

Because in this way, we eliminate the pathogens and at the same time eliminate the waste stored in the intestines that generates an ideal breeding ground for their development. Also, with intestinal cleansing, more pathogens are fought than with the classic Parasite Program thanks to turmeric, fennel, Lugol's iodine and oregano oil, which also help to eliminate bacteria and fungi.

**Must we carry out the classic Parasite Program as well as the Bowel Cleanse?**

It is optional and recommendable, but not indispensable if the Bowel Cleanse has been done. With the classic Parasite Program, only parasites and some bacterial strains are eliminated, which is why we consider it a better choice to begin with Bowel Cleansing and then carry out the classic Parasite Protocol (in case we have not eradicated all the parasites), although it is not strictly necessary and we can pass to the *Ascaris* Parasite Protocol once we have finished the Bowel Cleanse.

It is however important to highlight that if some part of our nervous system could be affected by parasites (multiple sclerosis, Parkinson's, migraines, depression, etc.) carrying out this Parasite Program would be of vital importance due to the inclusion in it of the wormwood that has a greater anti-parasitic effectiveness in certain zones of the nervous system such as the brain and the spinal cord.

For more information on Dr. Hulda Clark visit www.drclark.net

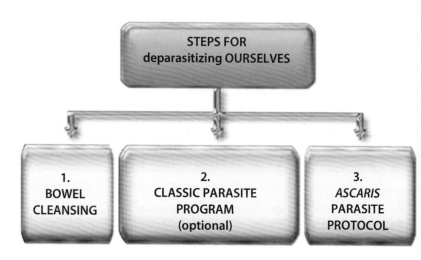

STEPS FOR
deparasitizing OURSELVES

**1.
BOWEL
CLEANSING**

**2.
CLASSIC PARASITE
PROGRAM
(optional)**

**3.
*ASCARIS*
PARASITE
PROTOCOL**

In parallel to the programs we can use the
VARIZAPPER for 60 minutes per day, to achieve a
better effectiveness of the parasite cleansing

## Bowel Cleansing

Many people identify the digestive system only by the colon, maybe because of the publicity that its cleansings have been given recently. But the reality is that health and the proper functioning of the colon depend directly on the stomach, small intestine, liver and pancreas functioning properly. The Clark protocol of intestinal cleansing cleans, regulates and eliminates pathogens from all these organs.

We will explain briefly how our digestive system works: the second phase of digestion, after chewing and salivation of the food in the mouth, begins in the stomach. But sadly it is there where a large part of our health problems may begin.

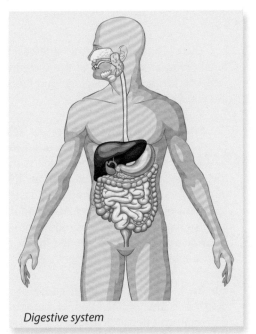

*Digestive system*

If our stomach does not produce sufficient hydrochloric acid (HCl), the food ingested will not be sufficiently healthy, since bacteria, parasite eggs and other pathogens present in the majority of foods cannot be eliminated by the acidity of the stomach. This brings about a conquest of our entire digestive system (intestines, liver, pancreas...) by these pathogens, with the consequent problems that this could lead to. We can say that the prevention and recovery from all illnesses depends on the digestive system, beginning with the stomach.

This lack of acids also provokes the incorrect production of enzymes and hormones by other organs. When our digestion is not working properly, waste is accumulated throughout the entire intestinal tract. This waste generally brings about the depression of the immune system and the proliferation of parasites, bacteria, viruses and fungi throughout the entire body. Due to this,

Dr. Clark recommended the use of anti-parasitic, anti-bacterial and anti-fungal agents in her intestinal cleansings.

For Clark Therapy, 90% of illnesses have their origin in the improper functioning and hygiene of the digestive system, which ends up being the reservoir for parasites, bacteria and fungi, so our health protocol begins with intestinal cleansing.

Problems such as the sensation of acidity or reflux are derived from the excessive proliferation of bacteria (from the food we ingest) in the gastroesophageal sphincter, which is the door between the esophagus and the stomach. This event causes an inflammation of the sphincter, which inhibits its action of preventing the gastric juices from rising from the stomach to the esophagus, that is, reflux is produced. Due to this, the use of antacids to calm problems of acidity or reflux aggravates the problem in the long-term, since an acid medium is needed in the stomach to kill the bacteria that swell up the sphincter and not otherwise.

For Clark Therapy, the main cause of symptoms such as constipation and diarrhea is the proliferation of pathogens in the colon and generally this derives from a deficit of acidity in the stomach.

Constipation is caused by pathogenic bacteria, more than by the lack of fiber in the diet. This is due to the bacteria excreting neurotoxins that interfere with the proper action of the neurotransmitters acetylcholine and epinephrine, substances that favor the peristaltic movements of the colon, which promote the emptying of the fecal material.

Furthermore, this excessive proliferation of pathogenic bacteria in the intestine also tends to be directly related to depression, since the neurotoxins excreted by the bacteria interfere with the serotonin (always lacking in this disease), denaturalizing the chain of amino acids that form this neurotransmitter.

## THE STOMACH

Most people with a burning sensation in the stomach or esophagus are treated with medications that neutralize the production of hydrochloric acid (HCl) because it is assumed that the reason is an excessive production of gastric acid, without realizing that alkaline substances such as bile cause the same sensation when in contact with the gastric mucosa. Therefore we deduce that it would be an error to think that the only origin of gastroesophageal reflux is gastric hyperacidity.

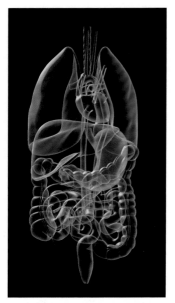

The reality is that the capacity of production of hydrochloric acid decreases drastically through the years, especially after 30 years of age. The stomach pH of a child is normally 1.5, while that of a senior citizen is 4. Since the pH of the stomach varies from 1 to 3, a pH of 4 would not be sufficiently acid to digest food well and much less to digest the gastric mucosa itself, which is the tissue that protects the stomach (as we are made to believe).

The real problem is insufficient regeneration of the gastric mucosa. In fact, in the cases in which this is very scant, the stomach ends up digesting itself, which is what we know as the gastric ulcer. The solution would be to regenerate the stomach mucosa (with supplements such as quassia or slippery elm) and

not reduce gastric acid, which leads to a worsening due to pathogen invasion.

For more information on Dr. Hulda Clark visit www.drclark.net

Furthermore, the esophagus has a pH of 6.8 and is not designed to come into contact with stomach acid. When the gastroesophageal sphincter fails to close tightly due to bacterial invasion, it produces a reflux, which results in a strong irritation of the esophagus, even when the level of stomach acidity is low. Then the solution does not lie in the use of inhibitors of the gastric acids, but in fighting the bacteria that cause the refluxes, without forgetting that bacteria have proliferated due to the ingestion of antacids that have favored a pH sufficiently high to allow the proliferation.

As important information, it must be added that studies of over half a century point towards most cancer **patients suffering from achlorhydria, that is, they do not produce sufficient hydrochloric acid.**

### Functions of hydrochloric acid:

- It is fundamental for the digestion of proteins.

- It inactivates allergens and neutralizes harmful substances present in foods.

- It is the first line of defense against pathogens that enter our bodies orally.

- It is indispensable for the proper absorption of minerals, especially iron and calcium. This is one of the reasons why the inhibitors of hydrochloric acid production, such as Omeprazole, can be initiators of osteoporosis.

- It is necessary for the proper absorption of thiamine (vitamin B1) and ascorbic acid (vitamin C), since these vitamins are inactivated in alkaline media.

Important steps in the digestion of proteins occur in the stomach, so if its performance is low, the digestion of proteins will be incomplete and two serious consequences will occur:

- Proteins will not be degraded to oligopeptides and to amino acids, but they will pass to the bloodstream in the form of antigenic polypeptides, which even in small quantities will set in motion a reaction of the immune system and the formation of antigen-antibody complexes. If these are produced in excess, they will end up accumulating in tissues and producing inflammation and tissue destruction. That is, so-called auto-immune diseases will develop.

- Most of the half-digested protein will not be absorbed and will pass to the colon, where it will promote gram-negative and putrefactive flora. This will fill the body with toxins and bacterial peptides that will undermine the vitality of the individual, predisposing them to all types of illness, including mental.

**There cannot be proper intestinal digestion if there was not previously a good stomach digestion. Deficient gastric secretion underlies many food sensitivities.**

The pH of the chyme (mix of foods and digestive juices formed in the stomach) must be acid so that the pancreas and gall bladder perform their digestive functions. When the chyme descends to the first part of the small intestine (duodenum), only if its pH is acid will the gall bladder contract to excrete bile and will the pancreas expel pancreatic juice, alkaline secretions that will neutralize the acidity of the chyme.

Pancreatic juice contains important proteolytic enzymes that have been forgotten by orthodox medicine. Their function is not only to de-esterify the fat and unfold polysaccharides and polypeptides. These enzymes perform an important anti-fungal function when they digest the chitin of the cellular membrane of the fungi and avoid the formation of mucoid plaque, a characteristic that is demonstrated in the cases of children with cystic fibrosis, whose first symptom is thick meconium (first feces eliminated by the newborn shortly after birth) – so-called *meconium ileus* – which produces intestinal obstruction since it cannot be excreted. When sufficient proteolytic enzymes do not reach the intestine, mucus is accumulated that covers the interior of the digestive tube and impedes the proper absorption of nutrients.

We see the intimate relationship between the various components of the digestive tract; when any of them does not perform its function properly, the rest is affected and a series of pathologies is unchained.

In addition to all that is said above, we must also know that the stomach mucosa synthesizes the intrinsic factor with the intention of it joining the B12 vitamin in food in order to be able to absorb it, which can rarely occur with the use of antacid medication, since they can destroy the intrinsic factor (enzyme needed to absorb vitamin B12) and cause anemia.

55

We must know that antigens are substances that promote the formation of antibodies (antibodies being proteins produced by our immune system when the body detects damaging substances named antigens), since our immune system recognizes them as a threat to the body. Most antigens are proteins, that is, amino acid chains. When an antibody joins an antigen, it always does so on the same link of the chain. This link is called an epitope. The immune system interprets substances with similar epitopes to be the same substances, and due to this the immune system may attack the body's own proteins by confusing them with food or bacterial antigens.

Another similar phenomenon is molecular mimicry, which consists of microbes adopting the same composition as their host organ to pass unperceived. The immune system recognizes them and fights them, also attacking the imitated bodily tissues themselves.

On the other hand, numerous bacterial strains contain proteins similar to those in the human body and if they pass to the bloodstream due to an excess of intestinal permeability, the immune system will unchain a reaction that will affect the tissues that contain the same proteins.

For example, ankylosing spondylitis and Crohn's disease are due to the presence of Klebsiella penumoniae bacteria in the digestive tract. This bacterium contains a protein that is very similar to the proteins of the vertebral articulations and the intestinal mucosa, and also produces an increase in intestinal permeability. These are two clear cases of illnesses caused by pathogens in the digestive tract.

## THE COLON

The colon is the most important part of the large intestine and its main functions are: to reabsorb water and electrolytes from the chyme (food mass emulsified and degraded by pancreatic juices and bile) from the small intestine to give consistency to the feces; recycle the proteins from the digestive juices; house the main population of the body's symbiotic bacteria; and eliminate toxins through its mucosa.

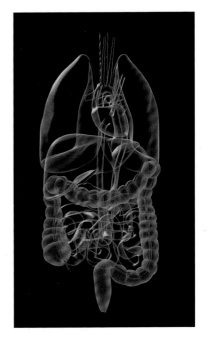

Some authors suggest that the population of bacteria that inhabit the colon is detrimental to health, but there are studies that show that this only occurs if the intestinal flora is putrefactive, that is, if there is an unbalanced diet that is low in fiber, consisting fundamentally of starch, animal proteins and processed foods.

Proper functioning of the colon is one of the pillars of health. Illnesses of the nose, throat and ears, feminine reproductive disorders, liver, vesicular and prostatic disorders are a consequence of an altered colon function in almost 100% of cases.

A. Bernard Jensen, US chiropractor and iridologist, discovered the reflex points of each organ in the colon and found that when one area of the colon suffered from diverticulosis, stenosis or another ailment, the reflex organ suffered disorders also.

From around 40 to 50 years of age it is hard to find a colon that is intact and possesses its original anatomy. This fact gives rise to the blockage of a large amount of feces in the colon of many people, especially of the chronically ill. And disorders such as chronic constipation and dysbacteriosis promote the formation of a lining of fecal material and mucus in the colon that become a source of chronic auto-intoxication and turn the absorption of nutrients into a difficult task.

The putrefactive gram-negative bacteria generate a large amount of toxins that overload the liver function and increase the toxic load of the individual. Also, its membrane contains lipopolysaccharides or endotoxins that exercise a very harmful effect on health. Lipopolysaccharides are capable of producing death due to shock and heart failure if they enter the blood in large quantities. This is basically what happens in a sepsis or blood poisoning. Luckily, this degree rarely occurs, but it is very frequent to observe a slight level of endotoxemia that produces metabolic symptoms such as diabetes, obesity and fatty liver.

**Studies on animals and humans reflect that the lipopolysaccharide blood levels of obese and type II diabetic individuals are above average. If we treat these people with the supplements that comprise Dr. Clark's Bowel Cleanse, their tolerance to glucose will improve, their percentage of abdominal fat will reduced, and their fatty liver will be at least partially reverted.**

**All who suffer from high blood pressure, prostate problems, asthma of a certain degree of severity or chronic constipation have a dirty intestine.** These people often exhibit constipation without being aware of it, thinking that their intestinal regularity is normal since they void their bowels every day. What really happens it that they are eliminating with a delay of more than 24 hours, with the feces corresponding to food intake two or three days previously.

### The importance of daily bowel movements

In order for a proper cellular detoxification it is fundamental that food does not remain in the digestive tract for more than 24 hours after its ingestion. This is because bowel movements not only eliminate remains of food, but also bile, cholesterol, bacteria, mucus and sections of intestinal mucosa. Many people even with a daily bowel movement are really excreting feces from food ingested more than 24 hours previously.

In order to achieve an optimal excretion of toxins, at least 2 bowel movements daily without straining would be ideal.

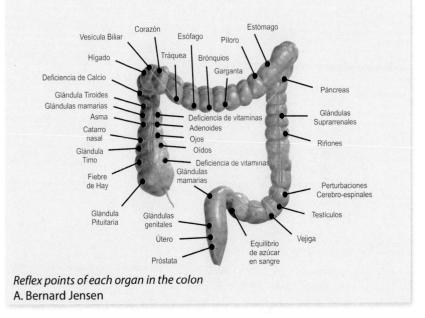

Reflex points of each organ in the colon
A. Bernard Jensen

Labels on figure:
Corazón, Vesícula Biliar, Hígado, Deficiencia de Calcio, Glándula Tiroides, Glándulas mamarias, Asma, Catarro nasal, Glándula Timo, Fiebre de Hay, Glándula Pituitaria, Glándulas genitales, Útero, Próstata, Tráquea, Esófago, Bronquios, Garganta, Píloro, Estómago, Deficiencia de vitaminas, Adenoides, Ojos, Oídos, Deficiencia de vitaminas, Glándulas mamarias, Páncreas, Glándulas Suprarrenales, Riñones, Perturbaciones Cerebro-espinales, Testículos, Vejiga, Equilibrio de azúcar en sangre

# THE CLARK BOWEL CLEANSE PROGRAM + OREGANO OIL.

**IMPORTANCE NOTICE TO THE READERS: In the following chapters you wil find described the different cleansing programs as proposed by Dr. Hulda Clark. It is important to notice that based on my many years of experience with patients, I have made some minor adjustments to dosages. Also, due to reasons detailed on page 47, I prefer to start with the Bowel Cleanse, whereas Dr. Hulda Clark would start with the Parasite Cleanse.**

- **Duration:  25 days**

- **Necessary ingredients:**

    - Black walnut hull tincture.
    - Turmeric (500 mg).
    - Fennel (450 mg).
    - Digestive enzymes (500 mg)
    - Betaine (350 mg).
    - Magnesium oxide (540 mg)
    - Cascara sagrada (350 mg).
    - Lugol's iodine.
    - Oregano oil

Note:  Oregano oil has been added to Dr. Clark's original protocol to increase the effectiveness of this cleansing.

**How to proceed:**

- <u>**Every day, at breakfast:**</u>

    1. Black walnut hull tincture (20 min. before breakfast, see dosage below).
    2. Drink a cup of hot water just before breakfast.
    3. Take 3 capsules of turmeric.
    4. Take 3 capsules of fennel.
    5. Take 1 capsule of digestive enzymes.
    6. Take 2 capsules of betaine.
    7. Take 1 capsule of Cascara sagrada.
    8. Oregano oil (5 drops in an empty capsule). Do not ingest directly due to the burning that it may cause when coming into contact with the oral c esophageal mucosa.

For more information on Dr. Hulda Clark visit www.drclark.net

## Every day, at lunch

1. Take 3 capsules of turmeric.
2. Take 3 capsules of fennel.
3. Take 1 capsule of digestive enzymes
4. Take 2 capsules of betaine.
5. Take one capsule of magnesium oxide.

## Every day, at dinner:

1. Take 3 capsules of turmeric.
2. Take 3 capsules of fennel.
3. Take 1 capsule of digestive enzymes.
4. Take 2 capsules of betaine.
5. Take one capsule of magnesium oxide.
6. Oregano oil (5 drops in an empty capsule).

## Between meals:

Lugol's iodine: 6 drops, 4 times a day, in 1/2 glass of water.

## Doses

Black walnut hull tincture: days 1 to 5: 1 tablespoon every day **in cold water**. Days 8, 12, 16, 20 and 24: 3 tablespoons every day **in cold water**.

## Weekly maintenance:

Once the Bowel Cleanse is complete, we recommend carrying out a weekly maintenance of:

– Black walnut hull tincture: 1 to 3 tablespoons in cold water, taken slowly.

– Oregano oil: 5 drops in an empty capsule.

– Lugol's iodine: 6 drops in ½ glass of water twice a day.

For more information on Dr. Hulda Clark visit www.drclark.net

# PROPERTIES OF THE SUPPLEMENTS USED IN THE BOWEL CLEANSE PROGRAM

**A. Black walnut hull tincture** (must be ingested with cold water because it loses its healing properties in warm or hot water; must be refrigerated, and consumed in less than three weeks, because once the container is open, its anti-parasitic effects decrease).

*Black walnut tree (Juglans nigra)*

Contains:

■ Juglone
  – Phytotoxic alkaloid. This means that the walnut tree produces this to avoid other plants from growing around it.
  – It not only attacks parasites, but also bacteria, viruses, and fungi.
  – External application can eliminate certain skin fungi.

■ Tannins:
  – They are anti-bacterial, anti-carcinogenic, anti-diarrheal, anti-hepatotoxic, and anti-hypertensive, are chelating agents, and act against tumors.
  – They are the plant's natural defense against herbivores, pathogens, and adverse weather conditions.

■ Iodine:
  – Antiseptic. Attacks pathogenic bacteria.

For more information on Dr. Hulda Clark visit www.drclark.net

Without a doubt, the American black walnut hull tincture is the queen of the anti-parasitic. To this date, there is nothing else that measures up to it. It covers a broad spectrum and is completely safe. Both the European black walnut (*Juglans regia*) and the American black walnut (*Juglans nigra*) are especially rich in phytochemicals with nematicidal activity (exterminator of worms that feed on roots). It is widely known that under the canopy of a walnut tree there are no earthworms or other worms, which is due to the anti-parasitic substances in the fallen leaves on the ground and in their roots. However, walnut hull tincture is not effective against *Ascaris*, or pinworms (parasites that very frequently colonize us).

Black walnut hull tincture eliminates the adult phase of many parasites, but does not effectively attack parasites in the brain.

The effective dose varies on the degree of the parasitic infection. One tablespoon daily for 5 to 7 days usually produces satisfactory results. It is recommendable to continue with 1 or 2 tablespoons a week for maintenance. This is especially important for those suffering from cancer or other degenerative diseases, as well as for prevention for any individual. The dose must be increased gradually beginning with only a few drops, because if the person is heavily infected with parasites, detoxification symptoms may appear. These symptoms are adverse reactions as a result of the bacteria and viruses that are released when these parasites die. These detoxification symptoms are in no case dangerous.

Black walnut hull tincture is also an effective fungicide, which is why it can also be used in cases of candidiasis. In this way it unfolds a double effect in this disorder, taking into account that Candida is also released by *Fasciolopsis buski*, which is also eliminated with walnut hull tincture.

People undergoing a program for alcoholism, or that suffer from acute liver failure, can be harmed by the amount of alcohol present in the walnut hull tincture – though it is minimal –, so they should substitute black walnut hull powder capsules for the tincture, although they are slightly less effective than the tincture. The powder capsules are not made from nut shells, but from the fleshy hull that covers the nut. It is the same part that is used to prepare the black walnut hull tincture.

## B. Turmeric

- Helps with hepatobiliary problems and hepatitis.
- Liver protector.

For more information on Dr. Hulda Clark visit www.drclark.net

- Prevents thromboembolisms and improves circulation.
- Helps reduce glucose levels in diabetics.
- Can control tumor growth.
- Indicated for cholelithiasis (gallstones) and cholecystitis (inflammation of the gallbladder).
- Effective anti-bacterial agent.
- Is a natural anti-inflammatory.
- Increases appetite.
- Do not take if you suffer from a stomach ulcer or intestinal hemorrhage.

## C. Fennel

- Is a carminative (stimulates gastric motility).
- Antiseptic.
- Mucolytic (dissolves mucus).
- Expectorant, with anti-tussive properties.
- Diuretic.
- Anti-bacterial.
- Contraindicated for hypoestrogenism.
- Anti-rheumatic.
- Promotes the elimination of bodily fluids.
- Useful in glaucoma, because it reduces the pressure within the eye.
- Stimulates digestion.
- Reduces blood cholesterol levels.
- Antioxidant.
- Used to fight anemia due to its high iron content.
- Stimulates menstruation and relieves the pains it causes.
- Helps fight bad breath.

## D. Digestive enzymes

- Digest the remains of the exterminated parasites.
- Facilitate the digestion of fats, proteins, and carbohydrates.
- Prevent the formation of intestinal gas, caused by fermentation of undigested food.
- Inhibit certain allergenic substances that are ingested through food.

- Prevent inflammation and hypertrophy of the various organs that comprise the digestive system, above all the liver, the pancreas, and the gallbladder.
- Stimulate the body's processes of detoxification and elimination.
- Help reduce pain and inflammation of wounds and traumas, accelerating healing.

## E. Betaine

- Eliminates fat from the liver.
- Assists in the digestion of proteins in the stomach.
- Helps with the absorption of iron and calcium.
- Increases the acidity of the gastric environment (which becomes an effective anti-bacterial agent at the stomach level).
- Provokes the secretion of pepsin.
- Improves the absorption of vitamins B and C.
- Sterilizes foods that are ingested.
- Prevents intestinal absorption of parasites.

## F. Magnesium oxide

- Regulates blood cholesterol.
- Regulates blood sugar levels.
- Helps in the assimilation of vitamins and minerals.
- Participates as an intracellular mineral that is essential for the transmission of nerve impulses.
- Participates in the repair and maintenance of cells and organ tissues.
- Helps organ growth.
- Fundamental in the processes of muscular contraction and relaxation.
- Stimulates the correct utilization of vitamins B, C, and E.
- Helps dissolve kidney stones.

## G. Lugol's iodine (Iodine solution. Do not use if you are allergic to iodine)

- Antiseptic.
- Efficient against bacterial infections, especially *Salmonella* and *Shigella*.

- People affected with hyperthyroidism, do not have problems when ingesting it because its effects in the indicated dose will in no way affect the thyroid gland, and its effect will be limited to the intestinal area. According to Dr. Clark, for Lugol's iodine to reach the thyroid, over 30 drops per dose would be necessary.

## H. Cascara sagrada

- Stimulates bowel movement. Since Cascara sagrada is a stimulant laxative, do not take it if you already suffer from diarrhea, or if diarrhea sets in after taking this product.

## I. Oregano oil

It has been included in the bowel cleanse program to increase its efficiency against specific bacteria and fungi.

Essential oil of oregano has generated great interest in the past few years given its efficiency, its broad spectrum effect, and its safeness. In Clark Therapy, essential oil of oregano is one of the main anti-infective agents used. It is especially useful against the different strains of *Clostridium* and *Streptococcus* bacteria. Chronic candidiasis, currently very common, is another disorder that oregano essential oil combats effectively. Additionally, oregano oil is a potent antioxidant. The best way to take it is by trickling it into an empty gelatin capsule right before ingesting. The drops must not be taken directly because the oil is an extreme irritant to the oral and esophageal mucosa.

The effective dose varies between 5 and 10 drops per dose; once, twice, or three times a day. Initially, one may experience reflux and some stomach discomfort. It is best to take food with it, and to increase the dose gradually. Oregano essential oil must be used in all the protocols that fight against infectious diseases.

Some of its most important properties are:

- Stimulates the immune system.
- Anti-inflammatory.
- Analgesic.
- Fungicide (eliminates fungi).
- Antioxidant.
- Anti-parasitic.
- Antibiotic.
- Anti-viral

# CLASSIC PARASITE CLEANSE FOR ADULTS
## (from 17 years of age)

- **Duration: minimum 1 month.** After the cleanse, a weekly maintenance should be performed in order to avoid reinfection or development of new parasitic infections.

- **Supplements used:**

  - Black walnut hull tincture.
  - Wormwood
  - Cloves
  - Ornithine (optional).
  - Arginine (optional)

- **How to proceed:**

| Day | BLACK WALNUT HULL TINCTURE 20 min, before a meal in half a glass of cold water Drink slowly (in under 10 min.) | WORMWOOD (365 mg) Take once a day | CLOVES (500 mg) 3 minutes after taking wormwood | ORNITHINE (500 mg) Before bedtime (preferably on an empty stomach) |
|---|---|---|---|---|
| 1 | 2 teaspoons | 3 capsules once a day | 3 capsules 3 times daily | 2 capsules once a day |
| 2 | 2 teaspoons | 4 capsules once a day | 3 capsules 3 times daily | 2 capsules once a day |
| 3 | 2 teaspoons | 4 capsules once a day | 3 capsules 3 times daily | 2 capsules once a day |
| 4 | 2 tablespoons | 5 capsules once a day | 3 capsules 3 times daily | 2 capsules once a day |
| 5 | Nothing | 5 capsules once a day | 3 capsules 3 times daily | 2 capsules once a day |
| 6 | Nothing | 6 capsules once a day | 3 capsules 3 times daily | 2 capsules once a day |
| 7 | Nothing | 6 capsules once a day | 3 capsules 3 times daily | 2 capsules once a day |
| 8 | Nothing | 7 capsules once a day | 3 capsules 3 times daily | 2 capsules once a day |
| 9 | 2 tablespoons | 7 capsules once a day | 3 capsules 3 times daily | 2 capsules once a day |
| 10 | Nothing | 5 capsules once a day | 3 capsules 3 times daily | 2 capsules once a day |
| 11 | Nothing | 6 capsules once a day | 3 capsules 3 times daily | 2 capsules once a day |
| 12 | Nothing | 6 capsules once a day | 3 capsules 3 times daily | 2 capsules once a day |
| 13 | Nothing | 7 capsules once a day | 3 capsules 3 times daily | 2 capsules once a day |
| 14 | 3 tablespoons | 7 capsules once a day | 3 capsules 3 times daily | 2 capsules once a day |
| After | 3 tablespoons (Once a week within 10 min) | Take only walnut tincture from here on | Take only walnut tincture from here on | Take as needed – it is not habit forming |

For more information on Dr. Hulda Clark visit www.drclark.net

– Take the black walnut hull tincture, wormwood, and cloves within 10 minute
   for best effectiveness.


– Once open, keep the black walnut hull tincture refrigerated (IMPORTANT) – i
you do not, it will lose its potency too quickly.
In fact, black walnut hull tincture begins to lose effectiveness a few weeks afte
the container has been opened, even if refrigerated.


Beginning on day 14, take the following once a week for maintenance:

–   Black walnut hull tincture, 3 tablespoons in a glass of cold water.

–   Wormwood (365 mg): 7 capsules once a day.

–   Cloves (500 mg): 3 capsules 3 times daily with a meal.

–   Ornithine (500 mg) (optional): before bedtime, preferably on an empty
    stomach: 2 capsules before bedtime. If you feel it helps you sleep, you can
    take up to 6 capsules.

–   Arginine (500 mg): Dr. Clark recommends this product if you are low in
    energy and drag yourself through the day. Take 2 capsules with breakfast
    and if needed two capsules with lunch. Do not take arginine if you are
    suffering from herpes outbreaks. Arginine is an antagonist of lysine, which
    can prevent Herpes outbreaks.

For more information on Dr. Hulda Clark visit www.drclark.net

# CLASSIC PARASITE CLEANSE FOR CHILDREN

- **Duration: 3 weeks**

- **Supplements used:**
  - Black walnut hull tincture
  - Ornithine (optional) (500 mg): 1 capsule ½ hour before bedtime (preferably on an empty stomach) until the jar is finished.

| Day | BLACK WALNUT HULL TINCTURE (20 min before a meal with half a glass of cold water) Drink slowly (in under 15 minutes) |
|-----|-----|
| 1 | 1 drop |
| 2 | 2 drops |
| 3 | 3 drops |
| 4 | 4 drops |
| 5 | 5 drops |
| 6 | 6 drops |
| 7 | ■ Less than 6 months old: ¼ teaspoon    ■ 6 months to 5 years old: ½ teaspoon<br>■ 6 to 10 years old: 1 teaspoon    ■ 11 to 16 years old: 1½ teaspoons |
| 8 | nothing |
| 9 | nothing |
| 10 | nothing |
| 11 | nothing |
| 12 | nothing |
| 13 | nothing |
| 14 | ■ Less than 6 months old: 1/4 teaspoon    ■ 6 months to 5 years old: ½ teaspoon<br>■ 6 to 10 years old: 1 teaspoon    ■ 11 to 16 years old: 1½ teaspoons |
| 15 | nothing |
| 16 | nothing |
| 17 | nothing |
| 18 | nothing |
| 19 | nothing |
| 20 | nothing |
| 21 | ■ Less than 6 months old: ¼ teaspoon    ■ 6 months to 5 years old: ½ teaspoon<br>■ 6 to 10 years old: 1 teaspoon    ■ 11 to 16 years old: 1½ teaspoons |

- Continue the maintenance with the black walnut hull tincture every 7 days or as recommended by a therapist

71

# CLASSIC PARASITE CLEANSE PROGRAM FOR PETS

(Quantities indicated for every 10 pounds of weight)

- **Duration: 4 weeks.**

- **Necessary ingredients:**

    - Parsley (necessary the first time Parasite Cleanse is performed, optional later on).
    - Black walnut hull tincture (on an empty stomach).
    - Wormwood
    - Cloves

**How to proceed:**

- First week (once a day):

    - 1 teaspoon of parsley water a day (put 3 bunches of fresh parsley in a pint of water, boil for 3 minutes, cool and keep in the fridge).

- Second week (once a day):

    - 1 teaspoon of parsley water a day.
    - 1 drop of black walnut hull tincture on food (dogs every day and cats twice a week).

- Third week (once a day):

    - 1 teaspoon of parsley water a day.
    - 1 drop of black walnut hull tincture on food (dogs every day and cats twice a week).
    - Wormwood: open a capsule and mix a pinch in the pet's food.

- Fourth week (once a day):

    - 1 teaspoon of parsley water a day.
    - 1 drop of black walnut hull tincture on food (dogs every day and cats twice a week).
    - Wormwood: open a capsule and mix a pinch in the pet's food (approximately 1/8 of a capsule).
    - Cloves: open a capsule and mix a pinch in the pet's food (approximately 1/8 of a capsule).

For more information on Dr. Hulda Clark visit www.drclark.net

- It is recommended that pets be deparasitized periodically every three or four months, and in between, if possible, to perform a weekly maintenance of black walnut hull tincture, wormwood, and cloves until the next cleanse.

On the other hand, we must also clinically deparasitize our pets with the standard parasite removal agents, which attack almost exclusively nematodes. Remember that with the black walnut hull tincture we attack almost 200 different families of parasites that common parasite removal agents do not attack, except for Ascaris and nematodes. In Humans, we eradicate these with the *Ascaris* parasite removal program, and in the case of our pets, we must follow a veterinary protocol that attacks these parasites.

For dogs, I recommend using injectable or oral Levamisole because aside from being an anti-parasitic, it is also a potent immunostimulant.

**NEVER USE LEVAMISOLE ON CATS.**

> **Parasite purging protocols commonly observed by veterinarians only attack a few families of parasites, so it is recommendable to also use the Clark protocol for pets if we want our companions to be in perfect health.**

For more information on Dr. Hulda Clark visit www.drclark.net

# PROPERTIES OF THE SUPPLEMENTS USED IN THE CLASSIC PARASITE CLEANSE PROGRAM

**A. Black walnut hull tincture** (drink with cold water, once open keep refrigerated, and consume within three weeks).
This product has already been discussed in the Bowel Cleanse program.

**B. Wormwood** (365 mg)

- Attacks the intermediate stages of the *Fasciolopsis buski*, which are producers of the tumor growth factor.
- Penetrates the brain and bone marrow easily, and combats parasites in these organs.
- Attack the larvae of parasites.
- The Chinese used to use it to attack the malaria parasite.
- Is highly toxic to cancer cells, but not to healthy cells (i.e., it is selective).
- When in contact with cellular iron, it produces a chemical reaction that releases free radicals that damage cellular membranes. Remember that the parasite contains large quantities of iron. Also, cancer cells need a large amount of iron to replicate their DNA when they divide, and this is the reason why wormwood works as an anti-tumor agent (a breast cancer cell contains around 15 times more transferrin, an iron compound, than a healthy cell).
- Very good results in leukemia, especially due to the extremely high level of iron contained in cells infected with this disease.

**C. Cloves** (500 mg)

- Attacks parasite eggs.
- Is an excellent anti-fungal.
- Has anti-bacterial properties.
- Is an antioxidant.
- Its ingestion can cause gas, this is normal.

**D. Ornithine** (500 mg)

When parasites die, they produce ammonia. Because this has a toxic effect on the brain, it can cause us insomnia and some restlessness. Ornithine helps to detoxify this ammonia. Its inclusion in the parasite removal program is not strictly necessary, although it is beneficial

74

# THE *ASCARIS* PARASITE PROGRAM

Also called the "Mop-up Program", or the "Ascaris and Tapeworm Cleanse".

- **Duration 15 days.**

- **Necessary ingredients:**

    - Co-enzyme Q10 (400 mg).
    - L-cysteine (500 mg).
    - Ozonated olive oil (optional, but recommended because it destroys parasite eggs inside us).

- **How to proceed:**

**Day 1:**

   - 9 capsules of co-enzyme Q10 (400 mg). If over 150 lbs. of weight, add 1 capsule more for every 20 lbs. extra. Take with breakfast.
   - 3 capsules L-cysteine (500 mg): 5 minutes before breakfast and lunch.
   - 3 tablespoons of olive oil (ozonated for 20 minutes): take before dinner. If it causes nausea, take only 1 spoonful. (It is not mandatory, but highly recommended).

**Days 2, 3, 4, 5, and 6:**

   - 1 capsule of Q10 (400 mg): take with breakfast.
   - 3 capsules of L-cysteine (500 mg): 5 minutes before breakfast and lunch.
   - 3 tablespoons of olive oil (ozonated for 20 minutes):
   - Take before dinner.

**Day 7:** same as day 1.

**Days 8, 9, 10, 11,** and **12:** same as days 2, 3, 4, 5, and 6.

**Day 13:** same as day 1.

**Days 14 and 15:** same as days 2, 3, 4, 5, and 6

# PROPERTIES OF THE SUPPLEMENTS USED IN THE *ASCARIS* DESPARASITING PROGRAM

## A. Co-enzyme Q10 (400 mg)

- Most effective against *Ascaris* in the brain, bone marrow, etc. (zone where most parasite removal agents are not effective since they cannot penetrate into these areas).

- Doubles the effectiveness of the immune system.

- Supports different enzymes in their function.

- Fundamental in the processes of breathing and cell energy production.

- Carrier of electrons necessary in cellular mitochondria.

- Fundamental for the health of the heart and brain.

- Also useful for:

  - Diabetics (stimulates the synthesis and secretion of insulin).
  - Periodontitis.
  - Chronic fatigue syndrome.
  - Breast cancer (simply taking 90 mg daily has been of great help for this disease).

## B. L-Cysteine (500 mg)

Cysteine is frequently used as a detoxifier, and is an amino acid that is a precursor of glutathione, the body's main antioxidant. However, cysteine in high doses is a bactericide and an anti-parasitic, and is even effective against canine leishmaniasis. The most effective dose is 4 g per dose. The drawback of using such large quantities is that they can cause nausea and vomiting. In the *Ascaris* program, we take two doses of 1.5 g, and in general, there is no discomfort. Dr. Clark recommended eating a piece of bread if temporary discomfort was felt.

Cysteine is especially effective against tapeworms and Ascaris.

For more information on Dr. Hulda Clark visit www.drclark.net

It can also be used to disinfect wounds and beverages.

- Is a sulfur-containing amino acid.
- It forms part of numerous enzymes, as well as glutathione, taurine, biotin and heparin.
- Aids in the elimination of mucus.
- Ensures the stability of proteins and enzymes.
- Helps expel mercury, copper, and lead.
- Protects against the toxic effects of radiation.
- Is an antioxidant in the presence of free radicals.
- Can convert into glucose, which is an energy source.
- Activates the immune system.
- Useful in strengthening skin, hair, and nails.
- Helps in absorbing iron.
- Effective against arthritis.
- Helps eliminate malonic acid from the kidneys.
- Must be used with care by people with highly acidic bodies and diabetes (because it can lower the efficiency of insulin).
- Ideally, it should be taken 5 hours apart from taking ozonated olive oil or Lugol's iodine (because these are oxidants).

## C. **Ozonated olive oil** (20 minutes)

- Attacks Ascaris larvae and eggs (and those of practically all nematodes).
- The ozonation lasts approximately four days in the oil. When ozonating, calculate how much oil you will need in those four days, ozonate what you need and ozonate a new batch of olive oil four days later.

77

# POSSIBLE DETOXIFICATION SYMPTOMS FOLLOWING PARASITE REMOVAL

Parasites harbor bacteria and the bacteria in turn contain viruses, therefore when killing parasites, bacteria and viruses can appear that sometimes cause so-called detoxification symptoms. To avoid or minimize them, prior to the classic Parasite Cleanse, carry out the Bowel Cleanse (as explained above), which contains anti-parasitic agents and anti-bacterial agents, and also, because it eliminates toxins from the intestines.

Possible detoxification symptoms are:

- **Flu-like symptoms (chills, fever, cough...):** the flu virus has been released.

  - Supplements recommended if these symptoms appear: Elder tea and *Oscillococcinum* (homeopathic remedy found in pharmacies) (1 in the morning, 1 at night).

- **Nausea, diarrhea, digestive problems, fever:** usually indicates that *Salmonella* have been released.

  - Supplements recommended if these symptoms appear: 6 drops of Lugol's iodine (if you are not allergic to iodine) 6 times a day in water, best without food.

- **Sadness, melancholy, crying:** *Clostridium botulinum* has been released and travels to the hypothalamus.

  - Supplements recommended if these symptoms appear: 1 empty capsule with 5-10 drops of oregano oil (with 1 or 2 meals).

# ELIMINATING PATHOGENS FROM FOOD

Now that we have seen how to deparasitize our bodies, we must also know the hygiene measures to take to eliminate pathogens that may be present in food.

■ **Lugol's iodine or HCl** (hydrochloric acid 5%):

- Fruit and vegetables: Use 1 or 2 drops of Lugol's iodine or 3 drops of HCl in each quart of water used to wash them. It is recommended that hot water be used. Let stand for at least 5 minutes. Boiling them at 212 °F does not kill the pathogens; this is the reason why hospitals use an autoclave at 250 °F to disinfect.

- Dairy products: put 2 drops of Lugol's iodine or four drops of HCl in each quart of dairy product (milk, yogurt, cottage cheese...) and mix well.

- Eggs: add 1 or 2 drops of Lugol's iodine in each pint of water used to wash them.

- Meat and fish: freeze for at least 24 hours at a temperature of -4 °F. The food Zappicator can also be used. With meat and fish it is difficult to kill pathogens by cooking them because although they are baked at 400 °F, the inside does not usually reach more than 190 °F.

■ **Food Zappicator:** place the products on the plate, connect the plate to the VariZapper and zap for 10 minutes. (We will discuss the Food Zappicator later).

■ **Full Spectrum Light** (which will also be discussed in more detail below): kills bacteria, viruses and parasites present in the food. Turn the light on between 20 and 30 minutes some 8 inches from the food to be treated.

For more information on Dr. Hulda Clark visit www.drclark.net

# THE TRUE PROTAGONISTS OF OUR ILLNESSES

Orthodox medicine commits serious errors such as denying the possibility for typical animal parasites to infect humans. However, reality shows cases such as that of *Dirofilaria immitis* which infects humans although it supposedly only infects dogs.

Another error is to state that there are parasites that are endemic to certain places of the planet. This is an implausible statement in the era of globalization where people, plants and animals travel all around the planet. It is also often upheld that there cannot be an infection with certain parasites that are transmitted through insect bites (such as *Trypanosoma* of the sleeping sickness or the *Plasmodium* of malaria that are transmitted by the tsetse fly or the Anopheles mosquito) without having been bitten by the insect. This is a serious mistake, because the infection can be contracted through numerous modes of transmission in addition to those officially accepted.

There are many ways of parasitic transmission and parasitoses are not exclusive to tropical zones. Also, the presence of a specific parasite does not imply at all that the symptoms associated with it are suffered from. An example is that *Plasmodium* can be hosted for years without a fever, and yet these parasites can be producing non-specific discomfort without the origin of the disorder becoming apparent.

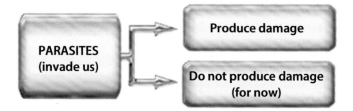

**Not everyone who is infected is ill in the present-day, but all sick individuals are infected.**

For more information on Dr. Hulda Clark visit www.drclark.net

Dr. Clark, as we have already mentioned, discovered that parasites are the main cause of viral and bacterial infections. Let us say that they are a type of Trojan horse that introduces into the host a multitude of hostile microbes.

The treatment of the pathogens must be addressed integrally and not with the short-sightedness of conventional medicine that, as we have already said, ignores the fact that most pathogens are simply the tip of the iceberg of a much more complex process. Directing our attention against one sole virus or bacterium would not be very intelligent, since the pathogens act in teams.

**Parasite cleansing must be one of the bases of any therapy that fights any type of infection, because we again state that parasites carry bacteria inside them and they in turn contain viruses.**

Numerous illnesses considered to be idiopathic (in which a known cause cannot be established) by conventional medicine are in reality of parasite, bacterial or viral etiology.

In addition to the pathologies already listed throughout this book, we must mention the so-called auto-immune pathologies that affect a large part of the population and are increasingly common.

# AUTO-IMMUNE DISEASES

Until now it has been held that auto-immune illnesses are incurable and that their treatment can only be palliative.
However, from the perspective of Clark Therapy, we will see that this is not so and that to the contrary, there is a path to avoid pain and suffering, that is, a path to health and to recover from these pathologies.

The commonly accepted definition of auto-immune illness is: "A disease in which the immune system attacks the cells of the body itself".

They are divided into two large groups: those which imply multi-organ or systemic dysfunctions and those which only implicate a specific organ.

**Examples of multi-organ or systemic auto-immune illnesses:**

- Rheumatoid arthritis.
- Some dermatitis.
- Behçet's disease.
- Scleroderma.
- Amyotrophic lateral sclerosis.
- Multiple sclerosis.
- Kawasaki's disease.
- Spondyloarthropathy.
- Fibromyalgia.
- Rheumatic fever.
- Wegener's granulomatosis.
- Systemic lupus erythematosus.
- Polymyositis and dermatomyositis.
- Psoriasis.
- Thrombocytopenic purpura.
- Sarcoidosis.
- Chronic fatigue syndrome.
- Guillain-Barré syndrome.
- Sjögren's syndrome.
- Systemic vasculitis.
- Vitiligo.

For more information on Dr. Hulda Clark visit www.drclark.net

**Auto-immune illnesses of a specific organ:**

- Alopecia areata.
- Pernicious anemia.
- Gastric atrophy.
- Primary biliary cirrhosis.
- Primary sclerosing cholangitis.
- Ulcerative colitis.
- Type 1 diabetes mellitus.
- Celiac disease.
- Basedow's syndrome.
- Addison's disease.
- Crohn's disease.
- Graves' disease.
- Auto-immune hepatitis.
- Myasthenia gravis.
- Primary myxedema.
- Neuropathies.
- Sympathetic opthalmia.
- Pemphigus vulgaris.
- Miller-Fisher syndrome.
- Hashimoto's thyroiditis.
- Uveitis.

It is most common to hear that auto-immune illnesses are caused by an immune system that "goes crazy" and attacks tissue. But that is not the real cause, but the symptoms we observe in these organ dysfunctions. But why does the immune system behave in this way? At this point, conventional medicine does not know what to answer and makes its excuses with the usual answer "...of unknown etiology".

**Biological medicine discovered almost half a century ago that the true nature of all auto-immune disorders is infectious in origin. Viruses, bacteria, parasites, fungi and protozoa are present in the genesis of these pathologies.**

For more information on Dr. Hulda Clark visit www.drclark.net

## AUTO-IMMUNE PATHOLOGY = PATHOGENS

**Is there a specific pathogen for each auto-immune illness?**

If a pathogen is present in a healthy subject without producing apparent damages, this does not mean that it could not be affecting the normal functioning of the organs in another individual.

The same pathogen may be the cause of two or more illnesses with completely different symptoms, according to the biochemical individuality of the subject and of the organ in which it is located.

However, in all cases of auto-immune pathology, as well as in many other degenerative disorders, we ALWAYS find bacteria of the genus Mycoplasma (which are not sensitive to most conventional antibiotics) and fairly frequently amoebas, Fasciolopsis buski, Fasciola hepatica, Clonorchis sinensis, Ascaris lumbricoides, as well as other strains of bacteria (Shigella, Streptococcus, Staphylococcus...).

In any case, there are many other pathogens involved in the auto-immune processes.

The different bacteria of the genus Mycoplasma perform a fundamental role in the genesis of ALL auto-immune illnesses, as well as in many other degenerative disorders. We can say the same for certain strains of parasites and amoebas.

In no case is there one specific bacterium or pathogen for each auto-immune or other illness.

We never find only one pathogen, but there is ALWAYS a set of different bacteria, viruses, parasites and fungi working together simultaneously. Numerous pathogens routinely present in the intestinal flora, such as Clostridium, Klebsiella, Escherichia, Proteus or Villanelle, apparently innocuous affect this type of process in a very negative manner. So, we can deduce that in these processes, strains of bacteria present in our bodies are implicated that have a specific frequency.

**Pathogens are capable of causing an immune response that affects the tissues of the host organism.** The mechanisms that begin this phenomenon are several, but three stand out from among them:

- **Superantigens:** An antigen is any substance capable of stimulating production of specific antibodies. However, a superantigen is a molecule produced by a pathogen that unchains an unspecific response and that involves a large percentage of lymphocytes and a massive release of proinflammatory cytokines, resulting in a huge immune response.

- **Cross-reactivity:** Most antigens are proteins. When a bacterial or viral antigen is similar to a body protein, it can occur that the antibodies produced to inactivate this antigen link to the body's own proteins and generate inflammation and damage to the tissues.

As we have already seen, the majority of the substances with antigen effects are high molecular weight proteins, that is, they are long amino acid chains. And when an antibody joins an antigen, it always does so on the same link of the amino acid chain. Here is where the confusion occurs, because the immune system recognizes the proteins by the links of the amino acid chain, not by the entire chain, that is to say it confuses organ proteins and antigen proteins. The pathogens are aware of this recognition mechanism and use it to pass unseen through the immune system. This defense mechanism used by numerous pathogens is named "molecular mimicry" and consists of synthesizing proteins identical to those of the tissue they invade. In time, the immune system detects the pathogens and attacks them, but it also attacks the tissue since it cannot differentiate them.

- **Formation and deposition of immune complexes:** when an antibody neutralizes an antigen it forms an antigen-antibody complex. These sets must be eliminated, since their accumulation in the body causes problems. Numerous bacteria and viruses produce antigens that give rise to the formation of immune complexes that are not correctly detected by the macrophages and therefore must be processed by the lysosomes (places where intracellular digestion takes place) of the layer of cells that cover the inside of the blood vessels (vascular endothelium). But once this defense mechanism is saturated, the immune complexes end up depositing on the tissue, unchaining an inflammatory response that destroys the antigens but also the tissue.

For more information on Dr. Hulda Clark visit **www.drclark.net**

# THE PATHWAYS USED BY PARASITES TO ENTER AND EXIT

## ENTRY PATHWAYS OF PARASITES

Invasion of our bodies by parasites can be said to be relatively easy given that they have numerous "entry doors":

- Mouth.
- Respiratory tract.
- Conjunctiva.
- Ears.
- Skin. Here we can distinguish two forms of intrusion:

  - Direct (although it is a barrier, some parasites break it: *Strongyloides*, *Ancylostoma* and *Toxocara*.)
  - Someone opens the door (mosquitoes, ticks...)

- Anus, vagina, urethral mucosa.
- Wounds and injections.
- Eroded mucosa (mouth or intestine).
- Cavities.

On the other hand, we must know in which way parasites can leave our bodies to have the possibility of establishing themselves in another and in this way preserve the continuity of the species.

## EXIT PATHWAYS OF PARASITES

- Anus.
- Respiratory tract.
- Saliva.
- Genital fluids.
- Blood and derivatives.

Once they have passed the entry barriers into our bodies, parasites multiply greatly in order to guarantee their survival as a species:

- An *Ascaris* female can lay around 200,000 eggs daily.

- In the case of *Plasmodium*, a sporozoite (stage of the protozoa during which it can infect new hosts) which penetrates a liver cell releases 30,000 to 40,000 merozoites (result of the reproduction by multiple division of the protozoa) when the hepatocyte is broken.
- Thousands of endospores from one *Coccidioides immitis*.
- Millions in the *Yersinia pestis* (bubonic plague).

It is very easy for parasites to survive since as well as feeding from "us", they also feed from products that form part of our ordinary food. We must also highlight that they can cause us serious vitamin and mineral deficiencies, given that in some cases they also need these nutrients to survive.

As a curious example of this consumption of food that is part of our diet, we mention some of the food "preferred" by parasites.

- *Ascaris lumbricoides*: the following form part of its diet: dairy products, cucumber, kiwi, squash, zucchini, melon and quercetin. It also devours vitamin B12 and iron.
- *Ascaris megalocephala*: any type of animal meat, including turkey and chicken.
- *Clonorchis sinensis*: oatmeal.
- *Dirofilaria*: lactose.
- Eurytrema pancreaticum: pineapple, lemon, chicken, cinnamon, coconut, raw broccoli lettuce, melon and pork fat.
- Echinoporyphium recurvatum: dairy products
- Fasciola hepatica: gluten.
- Onchocerca: corn and linoleic acid.
- Paragonimus: chicken, lemon, lettuce, pineapple, melon...
- Plasmodium (malaria parasite): wheat, chicken, lemon, lettuce, pineapple, melon, oatmeal, parsley, guava, tea...
- Fasciolopsis buski (parasite that causes cancer): onion, garlic, Aloe vera, asparagus, leeks, lentils, bread, etc.
- Gastrothylax (causes Down's syndrome, polycystic liver disease and cystic fibrosis): cinnamic acid from cinnamon.
- Strongyloides: potatoes, etc.

With this we wish to highlight the ease of these parasites in nourishing themselves and surviving within us once they have invaded us.

## HOW IS THE PRESENCE OF PARASITES IN THE BODY DIAGNOSED?

Currently, the diagnostic methods used in orthodox medicine as well as in biological medicine are incapable of detecting the majority of parasite infections, so in many cases the real etiology of the illnesses goes unnoticed.

We cannot continue to cling to the erroneous belief that a typically digestive parasite cannot live in another part of our body. Experience shows us that these pathogens can prosper and develop in the most unusual places: in the brain, eyes, kidneys, bronchial tubes, heart, in the liver, bile ducts, muscles, veins...

Although it is true that each pathogen preferably invades certain organs and is a parasite to specific species, this is not always the case and we must keep this very much in mind. Many parasites that are considered to be exclusive to cattle, to dogs or rats have shown that they can be transmitted to humans.

All of these affirmations are not the outcome of conjecture or speculation, but from conclusions obtained through methods of diagnosis such as dark field microscopy, the Syncrometer and the Dermatron (Dr. Voll electro-acupuncture device). These methods do not enjoy official recognition, but are doubtlessly very superior to orthodox methods and have opened a new path for therapists and researchers. The only problem with using these methods is that they require many hours of practice by the person who wishes to apply them. And of course the most precise of these is the Syncrometer (created by Dr. Clark), since with it we can detect any pathogen anywhere in the body with a precision that exceeds the detection levels of orthodox analytical methods. Thanks to the Syncrometer, Dr. Clark could carry out her revolutionary research and develop this marvelous therapy.

**Conventional methods based on the detection of eggs or parasites in feces, stool tests (cultures of fecal material) or serology (presence of antibodies in blood) are notoriously insufficient and do not provide a real view of what actually happens in our bodies.**

Dr. Clark discovered that each pathogen vibrates in an exclusive frequency and they can be detected in any organ of our body. They can even be detected by testing only saliva, because these frequencies are also recorded in our saliva.

*Ascaris*, for example, vibrates between 403.85 the 409.7 kHz, *Clonorchis sinensis* between 425.7 and 428.75 kHz, Herpes simplex 1 between 291.5 and 293.05 kHz, etc.

For more information on Dr. Hulda Clark visit www.drclark.net

Pathogens have their favorite places to live, for example the preferred organ for *Dirofilaria* (a dog heart parasite) is the human heart and that of an *Ascaris* is the digestive system. But in reality, any parasite can be found in any organ, especially if it is contaminated with solvents, metals or other toxins.

Clark Therapy uses a small sample of saliva to detect the presence of any pathogen existing in the body or in a specific organ. For this we use the Syncrometer which searches for the frequencies emitted by the pathogens and that are recorded in the saliva sample. With this device we can also specify in which organ, tissue or cell the pathogen detected is located.

Dr. Clark searched for years for the pathogens and toxins that cause each illness, developing a protocol for each; although we always have to bear in mind that there are no illnesses, only ill people, and that each case is unique, it is true that with a few natural remedies we can kill almost all parasites that cause the majority of illnesses.

**Clark Therapy has another point in its favor, and it is that with a few supplements it can treat almost all existing pathogens, because these cover a very wide spectrum of action and therefore usually it is not even necessary to know what specific parasites are infecting the person, since with cysteine, co-enzyme Q10 (400 mg), ozonated olive oil and black walnut hull tincture we are able to exterminate over 200 different types of parasites.**

Dr. Clark said ironically that since orthodox medicine uses different anti-parasitic agents for each parasite to be fought (trichloroethane, carbon tetrachloride, organochlorides, Albendazole...) and all are toxic, people with a large amount of parasites would die intoxicated by the large amount of pharmaceuticals before they were killed by the parasites.

Fortunately, in Clark Therapy we use only few remedies, never toxic ones, and they cover a wide range of parasites.

We must also bear in mind when cleansing parasites that by exterminating a large number of pathogens, this could cause the dead pathogen remains to overload our internal digestive capacity. Due to this, all anti-parasitic treatment must also be depurative, this is why for Clark Therapy it is always preferable to first carry out the Bowel Cleanse instead of the standard Parasite Program, which was the first one created by Dr. Clark, but which is preferable to carry out after the Bowel Cleanse.

89

## WHY DO WE GET ILL MORE OFTEN NOWADAYS?
## CLARK THERAPY AND IMPROVING THE IMMUNE SYSTEM

We have already seen how to cleanse the body of parasites and other pathogens. We now deal with the subject of eliminating toxins, which is the second fundamental part of Dr. Clark's health protocol.

The manifestations of an illness are only the surface under which we can find failures in different organs and systems of our bodies. In parallel to these organ failures, we always detect the presence of toxic agents in our body.

In recent years there has been significant and frenetic industrial and technological development, but attention has not been paid to the health of the living beings on this planet. Human beings as well as the various animal species are exposed directly or indirectly to a multitude of chemical agents, pesticides, fertilizers, detergents, medication, dyes, preservatives, as well as progress in electronics, magnetism, etc., which are harmful to our health. Most are toxic for us as well as for our surroundings, understanding the adjective "toxic" to have the dictionary meaning: "a substance that can cause serious disorders or the death of a living being".

Our food, the air we breathe, our soil and above all the water we use to drink, cook or clean ourselves, are full of toxins.

Our workplaces and our homes are surrounded with electronic and magnetic radiation from medium and high-voltage lines, computers, microwaves, cable televisions, telephones, Wi-Fi... All of these "toxins" act on our immune system, causing auto-immune conditions in us and an immune deficiency that explains the increase in recent decades of so many degenerative diseases such as cancer, allergies and other serious health problems.

Also, infectious illnesses that have not been so frequent lately are beginning to return, such as tuberculosis, venereal, fungal and viral diseases, as well as parasitosis with helminths and protozoa. And we must not forget the increasingly common problems of male and female fertility. So, the first requirement for the start of all these illnesses must be a state of immune deficiency derived from excessive organ toxicity. And we do not think that this state of immune deficiency only affects the terminally ill, but that most of us suffer from it.

For more information on Dr. Hulda Clark visit www.drclark.net

# WHAT IS A TOXIN?

A toxin is a substance that is harmful to the body. The effects that it produces in it are: an environment that favors pathogens, a blocking of the immune system, and a dysfunction of organs and tissues due to the great overload to which the body is submitted.

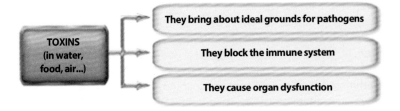

Since the arrival of industrialization, toxins have become more and more prevalent invading the air, food, water, cleaning products, personal hygiene products, etc. This makes it impossible to not be polluted; in fact most of us already are to a large extent. This huge contamination that surrounds us daily explains why there is an increasing number of cases of degenerative illnesses: **our immune system is overcome and cannot fight the pathogens that invade us.**

**Examples of toxins:**

- Malonic acid.
- Asbestos.
- Isopropyl alcohol.
- Methyl alcohol.
- PCBs, xylene, toluene...
- Formaldehyde.
- Benzene and derivatives
- Heavy metals.
- Lanthanide metals
- Azo dyes
- Chlorine.
- Radioactivity

For more information on Dr. Hulda Clark visit www.drclark.net

# MAIN SOURCES OF TOXINS

## 1. Water

In order to eliminate toxins from our bodies, the first and most important step is to decrease the ingestion of those coming from water. These days, almost all "potable" water in the entire world has toxins, such as: polonium, azo dyes, heavy metals, asbestos, benzene, iron cyanides... Moreover, in the chlorines usually used to disinfect water, Dr. Clark found: alpha radiation, antimony, arsenic, asbestos, barium, benzene, boron, cadmium, cerium, azo dyes, chrome III and IV, cobalt, copper, dodecane, dysprosium, europium, molybdenum, iron cyanides, methyl blue, nickel, palladium, PCBs, polonium, promethium, ruthenium, silicone, gadolinium, holmium, indium, lanthanum L, strontium, tantalum, tungsten and uranium R. Therefore, **chlorinated water is one of the greatest sources of immunosuppressant** substances, and as a consequence of this, the food that is irrigated and cooked with it is also.

In order to eliminate the ingestion of toxins through water one option is to drink water from a distiller, water that we will also use to cook with. (By this we mean that we will distill water using a homemade distiller and avoid buying it distilled, since in most water that is bought stating it is "distilled" we find heavy metals).

## 2. Toxins in the mouth

Along with avoiding toxins from water, food, etc. another step we must take is that seeing a dentist in order to replace the metal fillings (amalgams) with fillings that do not contain metals or toxins. It is preferable to go to a holistic dentist, since most dentists continue to hold the erroneous opinion that amalgams are not harmful. After water, it could be said that these amalgams are the second most important cause of intoxication. We will go into more depth on this subject later on.

## 3. Food

Nowadays, fruit and vegetables are normally sprayed with waxes, dyes, pesticides (thallium), anti-sprouting agents and anti-mildew agents; toxins that contain a large number of heavy metals, azo dyes, and malonic acid (main cause of degenerative diseases and renal failure).

In organic crops, we also usually find mycotoxins produced by fungi (since these fruit and vegetables were not treated with pesticides or fungicides). In order to eliminate toxins from food, we have the option of placing them for 10 minutes on the Food Zappicator, which is a device invented by Dr. Clark that neutralizes a large number of toxins in food (in the chapter on devices we will go into more depth about the Food Zappicator).

We must also avoid other sources of toxins, such as tobacco, toothpastes that contain toxins, commercial soft drinks, coffee, petroleum jellies, and cold cereals (common in supermarkets). We must avoid using the microwave and grills that oxidize minerals in foods, converting them into toxic metals.

## 4. Immunosuppressive medication

Most allopathic medication currently used contains immunosuppressive toxins. Among these are: analgesics, antibiotics, anti-mycotics, anti-virals, anti-parasitics, tranquilizers, anesthetics, anti-hypertensive drugs, hormones, anti-allergens, anti-coagulants, anti-inflammatories... Among the most important ones are antibiotics. Penicillin causes a decrease in the number of leukocytes, and increases the number of eosinophils that can cause hemolytic anemia and can provoke allergic reactions. Tetracyclines inhibit the production of granulocytes, thrombocytes, lymphocytes and interrupt the activity of phagocytes. Erythromycin inhibits the lymphocyte function and increases the number of eosinophils. On the other hand, most analgesics can produce leukopenia (decrease of white blood cells).

## 5. Pathogens and the immune system

A certain degree of systemic or localized immunosuppression is necessary in one or several organs in order for any type of infectious agent to develop and generate organ damage. As well as this prior immunodepression necessary for the development and activity of pathogens, we must indicate something that is not usually spoken of when dealing with immunodeficiencies, and it is the role of the pathogens as contributors to the immunosuppression situations.

**Parasites, bacteria, viruses, fungi and other pathogens cause in turn immunosuppression by direct damage to the immune cells, since during all infections free radicals are generated that injure the cells and among all of these also the cells of the immune system.**

93

While there is an excess of pathogens in the body – whether parasites, bacteria, viruses or fungi – different immunosuppression reactions are produced, among others:

- Alterations in the phagocytosis (elimination of pathogens and toxins) by the white blood cells.
- Reduction in the production of interferon gamma (substance produced by white blood cells to destroy pathogens).
- Increase in lymphocyte apoptosis (suicide of immune cells).
- Alterations in the C3 complement (an important part of the immune system).
- Decrease in the number and activity of white blood cells.

But maybe the most immunosuppressive effect is produced by parasites, since they generate or stimulate the production of inhibitory substances of the immune system. It is known that *Trypanosoma cruzi*, Toxoplasma, Leishmania, and *Schistosoma* produce substances to inhibit the activity of the complement. Entamoeba histolytica in turn produces inhibiting substances of the neutrophils and the T lymphocytes. *Ascaris* lumbricoides produces anti-lysosome proteases (remember that lysosomes are vesicles that contain enzymes to digest particles that enter the cells, such as bacteria).

Leishmania produces alterations in phagocytosis, alternations in the production of antibodies, decrease of CD4 cells and an inversion of the CD4/CD8 ratio, etc.

*Schistosomas* decreases the activity of the complement, causes a reduction in the production of lymphocytes, an inversion of the CD4/CD8 ratio, increase of antibodies...

But maybe most noteworthy is the serious immunosuppression that the concurrent presence of different pathogens within us can lead to, since some stimulate and activate the immune system and others intoxicate it with products of their metabolism. So, this duality of immunostimulation-immunosuppression, if maintained over time, will give rise to a severe immunodeficiency that is difficult to reverse in some cases. From this arises the importance of keeping ourselves as clean as possible from parasites.

## 6. Vitamin and mineral supplements

A large percentage of commercially available supplements are loaded with toxins and we can find chlorine and the rest of the basic immunosuppressants in them, if factors as important as avoiding chlorine in cleansing the packaging machines and of course only using high density polyethylene 2 or glass containers have not been taken into account in their preparation. In all cases in which these materials are not used or the lids of the containers are metal, we can be sure that those supplements will contain toxins.

**For this reason, we recommend only using original Clark products that have been produced and packaged so that they do not contain immunosuppressant toxins.**

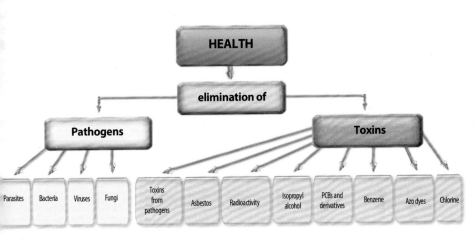

# STIMULATING OUR IMMUNE SYSTEM

We must be aware that our immune status does not only depend on the number of white cells counted in a blood analysis. It is very common that with white blood cells in normal ranges, between 5,000 and 10,000/mm3, they do not carry out their defense functions with the efficacy that they should, and this relatively common case is maybe what concerns us most in Clark Therapy. How can it be that a large part of the population falls victim to degenerative diseases, when their white blood counts are within normal limits? Well, simply because these white blood cells are intoxicated, and although they are within normal values, they do not work properly.

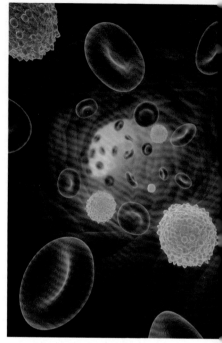

Orthodox medicine can see how many white cells we have in our blood, but not the toxicity in them. Through examinations with a Syncrometer, Dr. Clark realized that the white blood cells of practically all the patients in her clinic contained what she named the "five basic immunosuppressants," which are: benzene, heavy metals, azo dyes, asbestos and PCBs.

Of course there are other toxins that are equally dangerous to our health, but at the immune system level, the ones most dealt with in Clark Therapy are these "five basics", because they are detected at the immune system level of all, absolutely all of the people suffering from degenerative diseases and infectious conditions.

When our white blood cells are healthy, they can detect pathogenic agents and undesired toxic particles from a considerable distance through certain membranes that act as sensors. In the majority of the cases tested we find that our white blood cells cannot correctly perform basic functions such as the detection and elimination of pathogens and toxins in the different organs because they are intoxicated. On the other hand, our white cells have become south polarized due to the various heavy metals that they transport for elimination, when for their correct function they need a north polarization. When they are unable to properly get rid of toxins, their functions begin to fail.

The first thing we must do for our immune system in order for it to be efficient is to help detoxify the white blood cells so that they can unload toxins into the bladder and excrete them through urine. Therefore, they must be "fed" so that they can fight against pathogens and toxins. We always hear of immunostimulant supplements, but we must know that it is more important to detoxify our white blood cells, because if we do not, although we try to stimulate them, they cannot carry out their work properly. This means that it is very important to stimulate our immunity but even more so to eliminate the direct ingestion of toxins that make our defense system useless and to help these cells unload that toxic cargo that has "stuck" to its membranes.

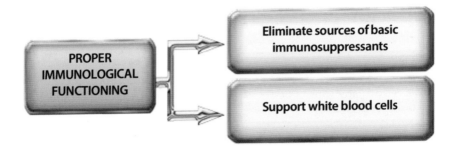

PROPER IMMUNOLOGICAL FUNCTIONING

Eliminate sources of basic immunosuppressants

Support white blood cells

# THE FIVE BASIC IMMUNOSUPPRESSANTS

**PCBs (polychlorinated biphenyls):** our white blood cells have their sensors placed on their external membranes, whose main component are lipids (fats). The PCBs dissolve this fat, and the white blood cells are incapacitated. These PCBs are tremendously toxic to humans and animals since they are also oncogenic substances, that is, causing tumors, and potentially harmful to the nervous and immune systems. **The most important source of PCBs is chlorinated water** and everything that has been treated with this water: food, soaps, detergents frequently used, plastics (except for high density polyethylene 2 which is the only non-toxic plastic and the one we should use to store food and water)... It is important to check plastic packaging of all the supplements we use (vitamins, minerals, herbs, amino acids). The plastic packaging must have underneath it a triangle with a number 2 drawn inside it. If it is another number, the product will contain toxins (this is what occurs with plastic mineral water bottles, since they are not polyethylene 2).

*Image of the symbol of high-density polyethylene, HDPE.*

As well as the neurotoxin and immunosuppressant action we can highlight other damage caused by these compounds such as hormonal alterations or learning disorders.

**Benzene:** this toxin is one of the main immunosuppressants and direct or indirect causes of diseases such as cancer or AIDS. Fortunately, the human body has a certain detoxification capacity for it. Benzene impedes the formation of blood cells; reduces the number of red and white blood cells; is carcinogenic and is the cause of myeloid leukemia; accumulates preferably in the thymus; is deposited in the white blood cells; and is found as a by-product of fuel combustion, in unsuitable water, coffee, Vaseline, lubricants, cold cereals and untested supplements. The quantities considered safe by official entities are not really safe, since traces infinitely smaller than those considered to be safe can cause serious damage. So these traces must not exist in our food, water, cosmetics, etc., since they damage us.

For more information on Dr. Hulda Clark visit www.drclark.net

**Asbestos:** this toxin has long and resistant fibers that can be separated and are sufficiently flexible to be intertwined, and also withstand high temperatures. Due to these special characteristics, asbestos has been used in a large variety of manufactured products, mainly in construction materials, thermo-resistant textiles, containers, packaging, linings, personal protection equipment, paint, etc. And we also find it in chlorinated water, sugar, fruit and vegetables, as well as in other food products impregnated with asbestos from what detaches from the conveyor and packaging belts.

Asbestos

As with most toxins, the size of the particles that we enter into contact with is not important. Contrary to what we might think, the smaller the toxic particles that penetrate into our bodies, the stronger the toxic effect. So again, particles not detected in conventional analysis due to being excessively small are equally dangerous and their immunosuppressive activity is greater. Everything that is "touched" by the asbestos inside us gets polarized south and, as we already know, the proper polarization of our cells is north. When our white blood cells detect the presence of toxins, they rush to "devour" them, since they are intruders. And when an asbestos particle, which has the shape of a needle, is devoured by a white blood cell, our body covers the points with ferritin, a protein that transports iron. When it tries to cover the asbestos points, the ferritin molecules break, releasing the iron they carry inside, which makes us manufacture more ferritin, so much that it ends us "smothering" the white blood cells, covering their exterior membrane, leaving them unable to sense and therefore unable to continue to detect more intruders around them, whereby they become completely useless.

Asbestos also has a carcinogenic effect and can be detected in a multitude of food products, as well as in driers and certain types of air conditioning.

**Azo dyes: present like the above in chlorinated water**, as well as in hair dyes and certain food products. They are carcinogenic and although they are prohibited for use in food, they can be detected in a multitude of products for human consumption that were sprayed with insecticides that contain them.

**Heavy metals:** of the group of heavy metals we can highlight: mercury, nickel, cadmium, lead, aluminum and titanium (although the last two are really light metals). The majority of heavy metals are toxic, while others such as iron, germanium and copper are essential for our bodies in their organic form, but are very toxic in their inorganic form. Their effects on the body are devastating, although certain health sectors have not noticed this yet.

**Among the things that are most polluted with heavy metals we find chlorinated water**, mineral water, commercial soft drinks, tobacco, unsuitable toothpastes, cosmetics, jewelry, metal cutlery and of course dental amalgams (which contain mercury, thallium, lanthanides and another 70 metals), as well as many medicines.

Among the countless problems caused by heavy metals, one of them is impeding the absorption of the minerals necessary for proper organ functioning, since they compete with them in absorbing them. They also cause hormonal, allergic, and cognitive disarray and immunosuppression.

Slow and gradual intoxication by heavy metals are more frequent than acute intoxication, but the versatile and very destructive effects they cause on our health have not been taken into account by healthcare professionals.

For more information on Dr. Hulda Clark visit www.drclark.net

# WHY ARE METALS SO DANGEROUS?

- Heavy metals catalyze oxidation reactions, and therefore, stimulate the production of free radicals.
- They impede the absorption of minerals and trace elements, which are necessary for enzyme reactions, and thus cause countless metabolic blocks.
- They can change the structure of proteins, and of course, of the antibodies in our immune system.
- Lipid structures, which are present in all cells, may be modified, so that the entry and exit of nutrients may be adversely affected.

Subclinical intoxication by heavy metals is increasingly becoming the cause of many health disorders.

Although the term "heavy metals" is very widespread, other minerals with a density of less than 5 g/mm$^3$ (density from which a metal is considered to be heavy), such as beryllium, aluminum or titanium, are also markedly toxic. Heavy metal intoxication can be defined as an excessive accumulation of metals in the tissues, which produce damage in our bodies for the following reasons:

- Interaction with essential metals due to electrical similarity.
- They form metal-protein complexes with inactivation of their function (also being able to affect hormones).
- They produce enzymatic inhibition of proteins with SH-groups.
- They affect the proper function of cellular organelles: mitochondria, lysosomes, microtubules...

Heavy metals compete with minerals given their similarity. They also replace essential minerals such as magnesium, zinc, copper, molybdenum or manganese, but are incapable of activating the enzymatic function, so the result is enzymatic inhibition and the consequences are disastrous. An example is Alzheimer's disease, which is characterized by an increase in the levels of aluminum in the body, especially in the brain. This results in an inhibition of the glycolytic enzymes that break down glucose to obtain ATP. Finally, the neurons do not receive sufficient energy, decrease their activity and finally die of hunger. This is only an example from among dozens of existing cases of enzymatic inhibition.

As an anecdote, we mention that in the eighteenth and nineteenth centuries, syphilis was treated with mercury derivatives. This illness was characterized by

101

the formation of chancres, which are contagious ulcers. These lesions although they did not involve a really serious danger, were alarming because of their appearance. It was discovered that treatment with mercury salts externally as well as internally, made the chancres disappear. However despite this relief, with the passage of the years the person became seriously ill and ended up with dementia and paralysis, which the doctors called tertiary syphilis. In the first years of the twentieth century, Salvarsan or 606 appeared so named because it was the number of the substance tested. This medication contained arsenic, which although it is not a metal, shares many similarities with the toxic metals. It was later discovered that the mercury salts and the Salvarsan were those guilty of the symptoms developed in advanced stages of the illness and not syphilis itself. For this reason, Dr. Peter Poynton wrote the book titled *Syphilis is a disease produced by doctors*. In reality, the terrible manifestations of the so-called tertiary syphilis, such as paralysis, tooth loss, dementia or blindness, were nothing more than consequences from the treatment with mercury and arsenic compounds.

Some of the illnesses that can be due in a large measure to intoxication by heavy metals are:

- Autism
- Schizophrenia.
- Multiple sclerosis.
- Alzheimer's.
- Parkinson's.
- Nephropathy.
- Cancer.
- Sterility.
- Hyperactivity and attention deficit disorder.
- Immunodepression.
- Anemia.
- Infections resistant to treatment with antibiotics.
- Degenerative diseases in general.
- All types of mental and neurological problems.
- Dermatosis.

For more information on Dr. Hulda Clark visit www.drclark.net

# HOW CAN HEAVY METALS BE AVOIDED?

First, it is important to limit the direct sources as much as possible, by attempting the following measures:

- **Avoid drinking tap water.** We recommend drinking water exclusively from the filter. Bottled mineral water is not a valid option because depending on the spring it comes from, may contain even more metals than tap water. Obviously, water from coastal areas is always much worse. Filtering jars are not suitable options either. The only acceptable system, apart from filtering, is that of reverse osmosis. Running water is a source of lead (especially if the building's pipes are old), copper (material used in many pipes), cadmium (used to improve the physical characteristics of PVC pipes), aluminum (forms as a result when alum is added to water to eliminate its turbidity). By adding alum to water, the suspended particles in it precipitate and form sediment at the bottom. On the other hand, many types of chlorine commonly used contain the five basic immunosuppressants, as well as radioactive particles.

- **Eliminate amalgams from the teeth.**

- **Avoid consuming large fish, such as swordfish**, tuna, bonito, shellfish in general, sea bass, eel, halibut, monkfish, salmon, sea bream, manta ray, and grouper. Fish with a lower amount of mercury are hake, whiting, blue whiting, sardine, herring, anchovy and trout.

- **Avoid antacids that contain aluminum hydroxide.**

- **Avoid clay dishes and kitchenware made with aluminum.**

- **All vaccinations are an important source of mercury** because they contain thiomersal, a disinfectant substance where mercury comprises 49% of its weight. Therefore, the annual flu vaccination so greatly recommended to the elderly, or the tetanus vaccination recommended to workers that are in contact with dirt, manure, or that are exposed to being cut by machinery or farm equipment, are frankly harmful.

- **Avoid tobacco,** since it is an important source of cadmium, as has been known for several decades.

103

- **Avoid use of aluminum foil or tin** when wrapping foods. Minimize consumption of chocolate bars, bonbons, chocolate eggs, and other products wrapped in aluminum, because large quantities of invisible particles from aluminum remain attached to the food.

- **Avoid deodorants and alum stones** that are sold in natural product stores, because alum is an ammonium double sulfate. The best deodorant is a mixture of water and baking soda because it neutralizes the acids produced by the bacteria on the skin, which is what makes sweat smell.

# THE PROBLEM WITH WATER

We have seen that the five most important immunosuppressants according to Dr. Clark can be found in water for household use. The problem is not the source of the water, but the chlorine that is added to that water. Dr. Clark, during her years of research, detected that the five immunosuppressants listed were found in all of her cancer patients. Other toxins containing radioactive particles were detected as well. At the end of her research, the doctor reached the conclusion that all five immunosuppressants were present in the chlorine added to public water.

The difference between those that were suffering from cancer and those that were not was found in two types of water, or rather, the two types of chlorine added. The most toxic kind contains potassium ferrocyanide, and is the kind that develops cancer in us. On the other hand, there is the chlorine approved by the NSF (National Science Foundation of the United States of America), which contains potassium ferricyanide. According to Dr. Clark's studies, this does not cause cancer, although it can cause other types of serious diseases.

In these chlorines, we find that their toxicity level changes depending on the geographic area. In Europe, those that suffer from cancer have ingested chlorine that is very high in polonium (radioactive) and azo dyes; however, it is lower in benzene and PCBs than other areas around the world.

All the chlorines used, that is, those approved by the NSF as well as the others, contain traces of polonium and cerium (a lanthanide element), which are the two first links in the chain that forms cancer. The difference between those that will suffer from cancer and those that will not, is contained in the third link, which is the particle of ferrocyanide (for those that suffer from cancer) or of ferricyanide (for those that do not).

In the carcinogenic chlorine, Dr. Clark found alpha radiation, antimony, arsenic, asbestos, azo dyes, barium, benzene, boron, cadmium, and other toxic agents.

### What water should we use for drinking and cooking?

In general, mineral waters are high in quality, but become loaded with toxins during the handling and bottling process. This means that the danger in consuming them does not come from the water itself, but rather from the toxins that were introduced along the way. We can make this claim because many brands that have been tested with the Syncrometer have the five immunosuppressants, as well as unsuitable chlorine particles that probably enter into the water from the bottling machines or from the bottles themselves.

For more information on Dr. Hulda Clark visit www.drclark.net

The best way to get high-quality water is to distill it yourself. And, of course, use HDPE 2 plastic or glass containers to hold it, since any other type of material in the container, including the plastic normally used for many mineral waters, could contaminate it.

Buying water that is already distilled is not a good idea because it also generally has toxins for the same reasons that mineral water does.

Why is the process for producing distilled water the best? Our goal when we drink is to hydrate ourselves, in other words, to get $H_2O$. During distillation, water undergoes a vaporization process in which it loses the toxins it contains, such as inorganic minerals and pathogens. It is then condensed and passed through a charcoal filter, which will convert it into pure water, that is, purely hydrogen and oxygen molecules. This water contains no inorganic minerals, which cannot be absorbed by the body; the only minerals that we can absorb are organic, which are those that are previously synthesized by plants or animals. The minerals present in non-distilled water, since they cannot be absorbed, end up deposited in the walls of the intestines, arteries, joints, kidneys, etc. The only living beings that can absorb inorganic minerals are plants. And, unlike what certain health sectors have claimed, distilled water at no time causes demineralization in humans. Water cannot extract from the cells or tissues any mineral that is part of their structure.

Distilled water will only cleanse the body of the inorganic minerals that contaminate us and that the body cannot absorb.

Regarding another criticism that claims that distilled water becomes more acidic as it comes into contact with air, we have to say that this is true; however, in no way will this cause an increase in metabolic acidosis, since this process fundamentally depends on the proper functioning of the kidneys and liver. Nevertheless, for those who so desire, this mild acidosis of distilled water can be corrected by adding 1/4 teaspoon of tested sodium bicarbonate for every 4 quarts of water.

Rainwater would be ideal for drinking when distilled; the problem is that it travels through an atmosphere filled with toxins, and becomes contaminated with those it picks up along the way.

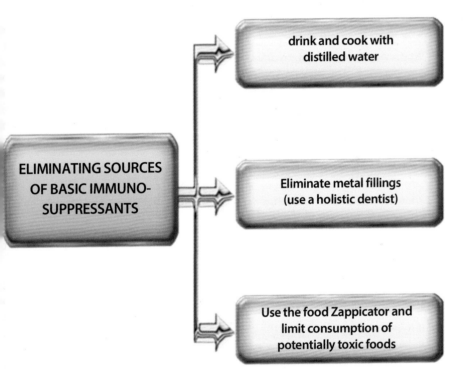

ELIMINATING SOURCES OF BASIC IMMUNO-SUPPRESSANTS

drink and cook with distilled water

Eliminate metal fillings (use a holistic dentist)

Use the food Zappicator and limit consumption of potentially toxic foods

For more information on Dr. Hulda Clark visit www.drclark.net

# HOW DO WE SUPPORT OUR IMMUNE SYSTEM?

Our white blood cells, as is true for all cells in our body, need food to be able to properly carry out their functions.

The foods that they need are:

- Organic selenium.
- Organic germanium (from hydrangea).
- Organic vitamin C (from rose hips).

When we use selenium, hydrangea, and rose hips as supplements, our white blood cells automatically begin to get rid of their toxins and start to work more efficiently. The best way to increase our immunity is by taking the three supplements together because they work in synergy. We take rose hips because of their high content of organic vitamin C and their capacity to act as an antioxidant of selenium and organic germanium, given their high flavonoid content.

Supplementing with selenium activates the discharging and cleansing of our white blood cells, which cannot cleanse themselves to remain active if they do not have high enough levels of this mineral. On the other hand, using organic germanium from hydrangea as a supplement, in addition to contributing to the cleansing of white blood cells, also increases the activity of T helper cells and inhibits regulatory T cells. It also increases the activity of the *natural killer cells* and the macrophages, while at the same time increasing the production of interferons.

It is important to note that the most productive source of organic germanium is hydrangea, since most germanium supplements that are tested contain traces of inorganic germanium, benzene, and asbestos, which convert good germanium into germanium that is not only useless, but toxic to our immune system as well.

We have to feed our white blood cells several (at least three) times a day to achieve the support necessary for their proper functioning. These supplements must be taken with food.

For more information on Dr. Hulda Clark visit www.drclark.net

Other supplements recommended to support our immune system are:

■ **MSM:** a powerful sulfurized immunostimulant that, besides being a powerful stimulator of the immune system, is also an excellent agent for detoxifying heavy metals and carries out the function of converting oxidized iron and germanium into good iron and germanium.
The recommended dose is one 650 mg capsule with 2 or 3 meals a day.

■ **IP6 (inositol hexaphosphate):** strengthens white blood cells and removes radioactivity from the body. At the same time, it is an excellent chelator of heavy metals and organ oxygenator. It is essential to remove the ever-increasing amount of radioactivity from the body—which is mainly caused by the chlorination of water and the materials used in our dental fillings and plastic devices—since these are used by numerous pathogens that, once radioactive, make our white blood cells not attack them.
As far as its stimulating effect on the immune system, the IP6 stimulates the activity of the *natural killer* cells and increases the production of reactive oxygen molecules in leukocytes when they are stimulated by chemical agents or bacteria. This is a defense mechanism used to damage pathogenic bacteria.
We recommend taking 10 to 20 drops with water once or twice a day, always between meals so as to not inhibit the absorption of minerals.

■ Along with these supplements, it is recommended to use the VariZapper for at least 20 or 30 minutes daily in order to stimulate the immune system, since this "energizes" our white blood cells.

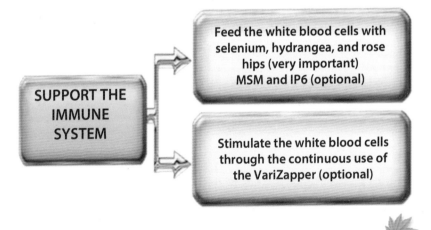

SUPPORT THE IMMUNE SYSTEM

Feed the white blood cells with selenium, hydrangea, and rose hips (very important) MSM and IP6 (optional)

Stimulate the white blood cells through the continuous use of the VariZapper (optional)

For more information on Dr. Hulda Clark visit www.drclark.net

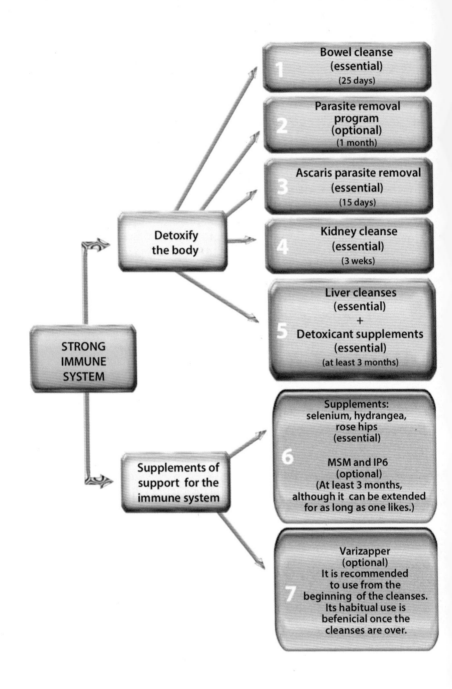

For more information on Dr. Hulda Clark visit www.drclark.net

more days). For best potency, you can also use new herbs.

2. Put 4 bunches of fresh parsley in 1 quart of water and boil for 3 minutes. Wait for it to cool and put 1 pint in a glass pitcher in the refrigerator and freeze the other pint. If you finish the parsley water in less than three weeks, make more.

3. Each morning, prepare: ½ glass of parsley water and 3/4 glass of herb preparation in a non-metal pitcher, adding 20 drops of goldenrod tincture. Drink this mixture throughout the day, never all at once.

4. Also take:

■ **At breakfast:**

- 1 ginger capsule.
- 1 capsule of Uva ursi.
- 1 vitamin B6 capsule.

■ **At lunch:**

- 1 ginger capsule.
- 5 drops of oregano oil in an empty capsule.

■ **At dinner:**

- 1 ginger capsule.
- 2 Uva ursi capsules.
- 1 magnesium oxide capsule.

# PROPERTIES OF THE SUPPLEMENTS USED IN THE KIDNEY CLEANSE PROTOCOL

### A. Black cherry concentrate:

- Excellent kidney detoxicant.
- Diuretic.
- Anti-rheumatic.

### B. Kidney Herbs:

- Strengthen the immune system.
- Help in the cellular detoxification of heavy metals and benzene.
- Excellent liver protector.

### C. Magnesium oxide:

- Regulates blood cholesterol.
- Regulates blood sugar level.
- Helps vitamin and mineral assimilation.
- Functions as an intracellular mineral that is essential for the transmission of nerve impulses.
- Works to repair and maintain organ cells and tissues.
- Helps with organ growth.

### D. Ginger root:

- Antiseptic.
- Kidney detoxicant.

### E. Goldenrod tincture:

- Kidney detoxicant.
- Supports kidney tissue

### F. Uva ursi:

- Excellent anti-bacterial for the urogenital system.
- Kidney protector.

### G. Vitamin B6 (pyridoxine)

- Helps with enzymatic synthesis.
- Helps maintain sodium-potassium balance in the body.
- Facilitates the dissolving of kidney stones.

For more information on Dr. Hulda Clark visit www.drclark.net

# LIVER CLEANSE

The liver is the organ that carries out the greatest number of functions in the body, wherefore it is also the largest of all of the internal organs, weighing up to 4 pounds. It is connected to the digestive tract through the portal vein, which means "door" or "gate" vein, since no substance enters the body unless it enters the portal circulation. The nutrients and the toxins absorbed during digestion reach the liver through the portal vein. The liver acts as a barrier that retains the elements that are dangerous to the body, preventing them from entering the general circulation and, thus, the rest of the organs.

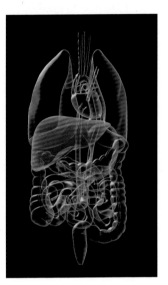

Among the functions it carries out are the following:

- It is a reservoir of nutrients, especially iron, copper, and vitamins A and B12.
- Ensures a constant supply of glucose to glucose dependent tissues (nervous system, erythrocytes, bone marrow, renal medulla, gonads, retina, and lymphocytes). This is due to its continuous capacity to synthesize glucose from stored glycogen, acetone, glycerol, lactic acid, or glycogenic amino acids. It is important to emphasize that glycogen deposits in the muscles, although they can significantly exceed glycogen deposits in the liver, are not available for the remaining tissues and have no influence on glycemia; they are used exclusively as fuel for muscular contractions.
- Metabolizes the hemoglobin from dead or deteriorating red blood cells, transforming it into bilirubin and storing the excess iron to be recycled later.
- Produces bile, a secretion that is indispensable for the proper digestion and absorption of fats. The acids contained in bile protect the intestinal mucosa, such that if the bile does not flow correctly, it causes a deterioration of the intestinal mucosa and the bacteria pass through this mucosa to move on to other organs.

Bile acts as a laxative and several toxins, medicines, hormones, cholesterol, etc., are excreted in it.

- Neutralizes numerous toxins.
- Regulates the levels of cholesterol and the resulting steroid hormones (estrogen, androgen, gestagens, corticosteroids, etc.) through their excretion in bile.
- Synthesizes non-essential amino acids.
- Synthesizes coagulation factors, which means that excessive bleeding may be an indication of an impaired liver.

**To improve liver function, follow these steps:**

1. Eliminate parasites and correct dysbiosis and excess intestinal permeability by carrying out a Bowel Cleanse.
2. *Ascaris* Parasite Program.
3. Complete a Kidney Cleanse.
4. Do Liver Cleanses until three consecutive cleanses yield no stones. Many people believe that doing one liver cleanse is enough, but this is not true since blocked gallstones require several cleanses to be expelled; only then will we observe truly significant results in our health.

    As the liver and gallbladder are being cleansed, we will carry out detoxification programs of heavy metals, cardiovascular protection, or the antioxidant protocol.

The liver is the body's laboratory, in which thousands of different substances are processed each second. It also neutralizes all sorts of toxins so that they can be easily secreted by the kidneys via urine or after digestion in the form of feces. It has the capacity to process an endless variety of toxins thanks to an enzyme system that can interact with a wide range of substrates. When the liver's detoxifying function is diminished, the functioning of the rest of the organs is reduced; indeed, no sick person has normal liver function. **There is no disease, except for congenital disorders, that cannot be relieved using a protocol for liver function stimulation.**

# WHY CLEANSE THE LIVER?

As we have explained previously, the main reason is to revive this organ's capacity to clean and detoxify the body. Likewise, in this protocol we also clean the gallbladder of any gallstones its contains, as they are filled with pathogens and are therefore centers of continuous reinfection. Even if the levels of transaminases are normal in our blood tests, this does not necessarily mean that our liver is functioning well. Make no mistake: these levels indicate whether or not there are signs of liver destruction, not whether or not the liver is clean and functioning properly. The most common scenario is that a liver is overwhelmed if no liver cleanse has ever been done, as we accumulate residue, pathogens, etc. throughout our lives.

Bile's function is not limited to only emulsifying fats in the intestine; it is also one of the major bacteriostatic agents (agents that prevent bacteria growth) of the digestive tract and, in addition, stimulates peristalsis. For this reason, people with liver problems or a lazy gallbladder have an overproduction of gases and constipation. If the bile ducts and gallbladder are not adequately drained on a daily basis, the cholesterol contained in the bile will settle and ends up forming stones, hindering further drainage and leading to a phenomenon called positive feedback or vicious circle. This process ends up producing cholestasis, which consists of the stagnation of bile flow, resulting in a state of hepatic congestion that affects proper venous circulation in general, digestion, and toxin excretion.

Behind many cases of dermatitis, joint pains, fatigue, indigestion, headaches, depression, sinusitis, hair loss, skin spots, bleeding gums, calluses on the soles of feet, under-eye puffiness, forehead wrinkles, and many other ailments is a congested liver. As a historical note, it is interesting to consider that the word "melancholy" comes from the Greek word that means "black bile," as the ancient Greeks knew that when the composition of bile is thick and dark, it affects the mood of the individual.

Stones form not only in the gallbladder, but in the liver ducts as well. The liver is not a hollow organ, but is made up of several ducts. Therefore, when a stone is trapped in the middle of one of these ducts, it prevents all of the adjacent hepatic lobes from being drained, with negative consequences for the entire body. The protocol used in Clark Therapy seeks to provoke an intense discharge of bile through the ingestion of olive oil and grapefruit juice to expel the many stones trapped in the ducts.

One of the supplements that we use in the liver cleanse are **Epsom salts** (magnesium sulfate). When they are ingested, the liver and intestine relax, thereby also dehydrating the different families of parasites. So, besides

119

cleansing the liver, these salts also carry out parasite removal in these organs. The liver cleanse protocol also helps to remove gallstones.

Why is orthodox medicine unable to diagnose the hundreds or thousands of stones that are accumulated in the liver? This is because most of the stones tend to have the same density as our tissues. To see them they have to be calcified, and for this reason they are not observed in tests such as ultrasounds, MRI, or X-rays. On the other hand, the stones accumulated in the gallbladder can be seen in these tests, because they are calcified and therefore denser.

**Tips to consider before doing a liver cleanse:**

- It is not recommended to do liver cleanses, or any other intense purifying treatment, if one has impaired kidney function. If there are any doubts, the home test kits to measure the urinary albumin are very useful for detecting kidney dysfunction early. Under no circumstances should a liver cleanse be done if urinary albumin is detected.

- Any treatment designed to improve liver function should not be carried out if it does not contribute to the excretion of gallstones and gallbladder sludge. Many treatments center on hepatocytes and do not consider the bile ducts. It does not make much sense to use milk thistle, artichoke, or *Desmodium* for a person whose bile ducts are obstructed by stones and whose bile is blocked by them. Most people, if they have not completed liver cleanses, will have part of their bile ducts polluted and clogged.

- Before doing a liver cleanse, the intestine should not have any obstructions. For this reason, 14 hours of fasting is needed prior to the treatment.

- We must try to avoid eating fats on the day of the cleanse for it to be most effective.

- Between 5 p.m. and 9 p.m., it is advisable to put your feet up or massage them because this helps to detoxify the lymphatic system.

- It is advisable to ozonate the oil for 20 minutes for it to act on any pathogens and parasite eggs that may be present in the liver, but if you don't have an ozonator, you can do the cleanse without ozonated oil. The properties of the ozonation only last for four days, so it is recommended to ozonate only what is going to be used in that cleanse.

- Do not do the cleanse if you are sick, or recovering from a sickness, because you will be weak and the cleanse requires energy.

- After a liver cleanse, try to continue emptying your bowels regularly to

For more information on Dr. Hulda Clark visit www.drclark.net

continue excreting waste.
- **People who have had their gallbladder removed can do the liver cleanse.**
- The presence of stones in the liver and/or gallbladder affects the equilibrium of the internal organs, which in turn may affect:
    - Heartbeat.
    - Blood pressure regulation.
    - pH regulation.
    - Hormone regulation.
    - Blood cell formation.
    - Sodium/potassium balance.

There are several causes of liver stones, and as we will see, all of us are or have been in contact with one or more of them:

- Intake of casein (dairy protein).
- Increased consumption of fructose and sucrose, even natural forms such as honey, molasses, syrups, etc.
- Fluoride intake: water, toothpaste, tea, vaccines, salt.
- Low amounts of sulfur-containing amino acids, such as cysteine, methionine, taurine, etc.
- Excess consumption of meat (especially pork), turkey, chicken, dairy, coffee, chocolate, citrus, eggs, legumes, nuts, corn, sugar, and soft drinks.
- Diet low in fats.
- Alcohol consumption.
- Constipation (when food spends more than 24 hours inside the body).
- Diabetes.
- Excessive exercise (due to continuous dehydration).
- Sedentary lifestyle.
- Excess estrogen (inhibits the synthesis of taurine).
- Rapid weight loss.
- Hormone therapies.
- Clofibrate intake (drugs used to lower triglycerides).
- Use of birth control.

# CONTROVERSIES REGARDING LIVER CLEANSES

The liver flush is a protocol that has been used in many cultures in ancient history as well as in present time. Dr. Clark recovered it and adapted it to her protocol, publishing it for the first time in 1993 in her book *The Cure for All Cancers*. Dr. Clark discouraged doing a liver cleanse without previously undergoing a parasite removal treatment and also suggested starting a kidney cleanse beforehand for best results, because during the liver cleanse a lot of toxins are mobilized and they can overload kidney function. There is no doubt about the safety of the liver cleanse protocol, although since it is an intense purifying treatment, toxins are mobilized and can cause numerous symptoms as a result of detoxification; that is, they are annoying yet positive for health.

An article published in the prestigious magazine *The Lancet* in 2005 caused some confusion. This article discussed the case of a woman who, following the advice of her naturopathic doctor, drank lemon juice with 600 ml of olive oil and, to check the effectiveness of the therapy, took the excreted stones for analysis. The results of this analysis indicated that these excretions were not gallstones, but the salts created from the fatty acids in the oil she had drank. From that point, several "experts" started saying that the liver cleanse was a fraud.

If we analyze the article thoroughly, we can see that the protocol that the woman followed was nothing like the protocol used in Clark Therapy to cleanse the liver and gallbladder. First, the protocol says to use Epsom salts, since they are a powerful cholagogue, in order to purge the intestines and dilate the bile ducts. Secondly, the protocol says to combine grapefruit juice and olive oil. This is because grapefruit has an effect that is very different from lemon, as lemon causes the bile duct to constrict, while grapefruit does not. Thirdly, the protocol says to use 160 milliliters of olive oil and not 600. It seems obvious that with this intake, most of the oil is neither digested nor absorbed; instead, it forms soaps in the digestive tract. In addition, once one does a certain number of liver cleanses (this depends on the person), their bile and gallbladder ducts are freed; no more stones are removed even if more cleanses are done.

For more information on Dr. Hulda Clark visit **www.drclark.net**

Several people have taken their stones for analysis privately and the results show that their composition matches that of the stones removed surgically.

# PROTOCOL FOR LIVER CLEANSES

- **Duration: One day.**

- **Utensils needed:**

  - 1 medium-sized coffee cup (approximately 1 cup)
  - 1 container of one quart and another of a pint (both with lids).

- **Ingredients needed:**

  - Epsom salts (4 tablespoons) or 60 capsules (965 mg).
  - Olive oil (½ cup). If possible, ozonated (20 minutes).
  - Grapefruit (1 large or 2 small: the juice should fill 3/4 of a cup).
  - Ornithine (if you sleep well, 4 capsules; otherwise 8 capsules).
  - Black walnut hull tincture: 10 to 20 drops.

- **Hints for the liver flush:**

  - **Do not omit any ingredients.**
  - Do not do the cleanse if you are sick or constipated.
  - Do it when you have a day off, without leaving the house, since you are going to pass several bowel movements.
  - During the two days that follow, do not take any type of supplement (vitamins, etc.)
  - Day one: from the moment you wake up until 2 p.m., eat only light, fat-free foods: fruit, vegetables, rice, pasta, etc.
  - Starting at 2 p.m., do not eat or drink ANYTHING.
  - Optional: you can put the mixture of Epsom salts and water in the refrigerator to lessen the bitter taste of the salts. You can also rinse your mouth out without swallowing the water after every sip. The option of taking the salts in capsules is the best for people who do not like the taste of the salts.
  - If you suffer from any degenerative brain or spinal cord disease, replace the grapefruit juice with a combination of natural, freshly-made apple juice (from golden or red delicious apples), ½ teaspoon of citric acid, and the oil.

For more information on Dr. Hulda Clark visit www.drclark.net

## Method of preparation:

- **3:00 p.m.:** mix and dissolve 4 tablespoons of Epsom salts in 3 cups of water (approximately 250 cc per cup) and put them in a 1-quart pitcher with a lid (enough for 4 doses of 3/4 cups each).
- **7:00 p.m.:** 1st dose of 3/4 cup of the mixture of Epsom salts, or 15 capsules with 1 cup of water.
- **9:00 p.m.:** 2nd dose of 3/4 cup of the mixture of Epsom salts and water, or 15 capsules with 1 cup of water (even if you have not eaten anything since 2:00 p.m., you will not be hungry).
- **10:45 p.m.:** put half a cup of olive oil in a container with a lid.
  Wash with hot water, dry, and squeeze the grapefruit, removing the pulp with a fork. The juice of a lemon can be added. Shake well to mix all ingredients until a watery solution forms. Also add 10 to 20 drops of black walnut hull tincture. Go to the bathroom before drinking this mixture.
- **11:00 p.m.:** drink the mixture that you just prepared and take 4 to 8 capsules of ornithine.
  Lie down immediately. If you don't, you will expel fewer stones. Try laying on your back with your head raised for at least half an hour, sleep in the position you want, and do not get up during the night unless it is strictly necessary.
- **When you wake up** (not before 7 a.m.): 3rd dose of 3/4 cup of the mixture of Epsom salts and water, or 15 capsules with one glass of water.
  If you feel poorly when you wake up, do not take this dose until you feel better. You can lie back down.
- **9:00 a.m.** (or **2 hours after the 3rd dose**): 4th and final dose of 3/4 cup of the mixture of Epsom salts and water, or 15 capsules with 1 glass of water. You can lie back down if you want.
- **11:00 a.m.** (or **2 hours after the 4th dose**): you can eat now. First drink a fruit juice, then eat fruit a half-hour later. One hour later, eat a light lunch.
- You will feel completely recovered by dinner.

It is normal to have several bowel movements throughout the day.
Allow between two and three weeks between liver cleanses for greatest effectiveness.
You can space them out more, but Dr. Clark always believed that more waste and liver stones will be removed if you do not allow more than three weeks to pass between cleanses, for the first three or four cleanses. However, they will be equally valid if even they are more spaced out.

125

# ELIMINATION OF TOXINS

This is our last phase in the protocol, to be carried out after the kidney cleanse and at the same time as the liver cleanses. Each time you carry out a liver flush, we recommend not taking supplements for a couple of days, in order to then continue with the supplements after each cleanse.

When the organ toxins exceed the capacity of the emunctory organs and these begin to function poorly, the body becomes progressively loaded with toxins and the organs' functioning slowly degrades.

Toxins surrounding white blood cells hinder the development of these cells' disease-fighting capabilities.
It has been confirmed that some heavy metals are the cause of specific symptoms and diseases. For example, copper appears to be the cause of the typical brown spots that appear as we age; cobalt causes heart problems; vanadium alters the production of antibodies and red blood cells; germanium oxide causes a deficiency of white blood cells; chromium causes problem in the regulation of blood sugar and pain; gold is associated with ovarian diseases, diabetes, and obesity; nickel brings recurrent infections, hair loss, and allergies; gold and nickel stop the flow of two of our main neurotransmitters (acetylcholine and epinephrine); aluminum is directly related to the Herpes virus and the Epstein-Barr virus, which cause chronic fatigue, migraines and Alzheimer's disease, etc.

For more information on Dr. Hulda Clark visit www.drclark.net

# DETOXIFICATION PROGRAM FOR HEAVY METALS AND OTHER TOXINS

- **Duration: 100 days, although it can be extended for as long as one likes.**

- **Ingredients needed:**

  — Vitamin B6: take 1 capsule at breakfast.
  — Vitamin C (ascorbic acid): take 1 capsule at breakfast and 1 at lunch.
  — Vitamin E: take 1 capsule at breakfast.
  — Calcium: take 1 capsule at dinner.
  — Selenium: take 1 capsule at dinner.
  — Zinc: take 1 capsule at lunch.
  — Cysteine: take 1 capsule at lunch and another at dinner.
  — Methionine: take 1 capsule at dinner.
  — Vitamin B complex: take 1 capsule at lunch.
  — MSM (methyl-sulphonyl-methane): take 1 capsule at breakfast, another at lunch, and another at dinner.
  — Alpha-lipoic-acid (thioctic acid): take 1 capsule at breakfast.

Take the capsules with a glass of cold water during or after meals.

## SUPPLEMENTS FOR DETOXIFICATION OF HEAVY METALS AND OTHER TOXINS

- **MSM** (methyl-sulphonyl-methane): it is an organic form of sulfur. It is a source of sulfur chelate, which makes heavy metals soluble. MSM works mainly at the extracellular level. It was the preferred supplement of Dr. Clark. I asked her on one occasion which, of all of the supplements used in her therapy, she would choose if she could only choose one, and she emphatically stated without hesitation that it would be MSM. Take 1 capsule at breakfast, 1 at lunch, and 1 at dinner.

### Properties:

  — Helps in the removal of asbestos from the body.
  — Increases cellular permeability: this leads to greater removal of toxins and greater absorption of vitamins and minerals.
  — A powerful antioxidant.
  — Deactivates toxins and enables their removal.
  — One of the few antioxidants that crosses the blood-brain barrier (protecting against excessive oxidation in the brain).

127

— Promotes mental agility and concentration.
— Reduces anxiety and depression.
— Lessens allergic reactions.
— Regulates autoimmune processes.
— Effective protection against cancer.
— Acts against fungi, bacteria, and parasites.
— Especially good for children.
— Reduces degeneration and inflammation in arthritis.
— Marked effectiveness in muscle pains and cramps.
— Similar effectiveness to aspirin or codeine as an analgesic.
— Regarding gastritis with hyperacidity, the use of antacids and H blockers can be reduced and even stopped.
— Increases oxygen absorption: by increasing the elasticity of lung tissu and inhibiting the agglomeration of erythrocytes, they are able t absorb more oxygen.
— Beneficial for the skin and hair (acne, eczema, dryness, etc.)
— Dosage: 1 to 3 capsules with a cup of water (20 minutes before meals).

■ **Vitamin B6:** helps to remove aluminum.

■ **Vitamin C (ascorbic acid):** this is the detoxicant *par excellence* and effective in cases of acute and chronic intoxications. In high doses, stimulates the liver's enzyme system, which detoxifies the blood an removes toxins such as heavy metals and pesticides. It also protects agains the increased oxidative stress resulting from heavy metal intoxication. It also an excellent protector against the dangerous mycotoxins present i many foods.

■ **Vitamin E:** protects against toxic aluminum. It prevents the accumulatio of lead in our connective tissue and lowers the toxic load of our cells.

■ **Calcium:** hinders the absorption of aluminum in our body and reduces th absorption of lead, cadmium, mercury, and the dangerous strontium-90.

■ **Selenium:** should be a part of every nutritional program intended t reduce the amount of heavy metals, since it imparts antioxidant powe tothe body due to it being a co-factor of the glutathione peroxidas enzyme and because it forms selenoproteins that react with metals.
The excess of metals in the body drastically reduces the concentration o selenoproteins in the tissues, which damages the DNA and provoke oxidative stress, among other dysfunctions. Furthermore, selenium has protective effect against aluminum, cadmium, arsenic, and mercury

reducing toxicity and oxidative stress.

- **Zinc:** reduces the toxicity of aluminum and the cellular damage it causes. Protects against lead, preventing it from intruding and affecting the enzymatic reactions. The presence of cadmium often causes a zinc deficiency.

- **Cysteine and methionine:** these are amino acids that contain sulfur in their chemical structure. Heavy metals react with sulfur, and it is only through this interaction that they become soluble and thus able to be eliminated by the liver and kidneys. Additionally, it helps vitamin B6 in its chelating effects.

- **Alpha-lipoic-acid (thioctic acid):** a saturated fatty acid that contains two sulfur atoms in its structure. It has a chelating effect like MSM, but is a fat soluble molecule that has access to almost all of the body's tissues and also works at the cellular level. It not only increases the excretion of heavy metals, but also contributes to overcoming one of the main effects of heavy metal intoxication, since these greatly inhibit the body's antioxidant defenses by reacting with molecules containing sulfur (thiols) such as cysteine, glutathione, and the cysteine-rich metalloproteins. Alpha-lipoic-acid is one of the principal chelating agents used in the protocol, because it crosses the blood-brain barrier and decreases the levels of mercury, lead, and other metals in the brain. However, it does not appear to be effective against lead. It is also a potent antioxidant and protects brain tissue from the toxic effects of metals.

- **Vitamin B complex:** we have already taken a look at the role that vitamin B6 plays in helping to eliminate aluminum. Additionally, vitamin B2 detoxifies benzene, chlorine, isopropyl alcohol, PCBs, toluene, and xylene. Vitamin B3 helps us to eliminate formaldehyde. Folic acid also helps to excrete formaldehyde, as well as the PCBs and malonic acid. Vitamin B12 has a detoxifying effect for PCBs, xylene, toluene, formaldehyde, and malonic acid.

129

# ANOTHER ENEMY OF OUR HEALTH: OXIDATIVE STRESS

When we bite into an apple and leave it out in the air for a few minutes we can observe that it begins to turn brown. This is what is known as oxidation. This process, in which oxygen leaves its mark, occurs on a continuous basis and is more noticeable in some things than in others, for example in metals.

This process also takes place in our bodies, since we metabolize the equivalent of about 18 tons of liquid oxygen over the course of our lives.

We need oxygen so that our mitochondria (our cells' "power plants") can produce energy, but 10 percent of this oxygen becomes dangerously unstable since it contains a free electron. These dangerous molecules are called "free radicals," which are made up of atoms or molecules that are missing an electron in their shells and are highly reactive because they travel throughout our entire body searching for molecules from which they can steal the electron they need to be complete.

In order for this continuous oxidation to not affect homeostasis and lead to an oxidized environment, the body has enzymatic and non-enzymatic antioxidant systems. But when the production of free radicals exceeds the capacity of the body's antioxidant defenses, "oxidative stress" is produced, which causes premature aging. Oxidative stress is the result of an excessive formation of free radicals and a reduction in the activity of the body's antioxidant defense systems.

Some factors promoting the excessive formation of free radicals include solar radiation, certain drugs, an inadequate diet, lack of exercise, and stress.

We all need to consume antioxidants to prevent premature aging and the degeneration of our DNA, cells, blood, connective tissue, immune system, organs, etc.

All bodily tissue is protected by different antioxidants.

The structures that contain lipids (fats) are protected mainly by the fat-soluble vitamins A and E.

Meanwhile, the blood, as well as bodily and intracellular fluids are protected by vitamin C.

Glutathione, a peptide made up of three different amino acids, is one of the most effective shields against free radicals inside the cell. Furthermore, the trace elements zinc and selenium are essential for preventing oxidation in our enzyme system.

We could get some of these antioxidants directly from plants, fruit, and vegetables, but we would need to ingest large amounts to achieve the desired effect.

For example, we would have to eat approximately 18 lbs. of oranges per day

For more information on Dr. Hulda Clark visit www.drclark.net

to consume the required 3 grams of vitamin C. Also, when foods are cooked, most of their antioxidants decay, making it even more difficult to get them with your diet.

We have also seen that antioxidants work as a team, which means that they have a greater effect when taken as a group than when only one is taken.

There are oxidative dietary factors that can lead to a greater need for antioxidants, such as:

— Overconsumption of polyunsaturated fatty acids, including omega-3, since these are very susceptible to oxidation due to the presence of double bonds.
— A diet based on carbohydrates.
— Excessive consumption of fructose, including from fruit, honey, and molasses. Fructose is ten times more prone to glycation than is glucose. The end products of advanced glycation, such as fructosamine, glucosepane, glycated hemoglobin, etc., are a major cause of tissue aging and damage. It is true that fruit provides antioxidants, that is, ingesting them produces reductive capacity in the blood plasma, due to the increase in uric acid resulting from the phosphatation of fructose in the liver. Fructose, in order to be metabolized, has to become fructose-1-phosphate, which comes from ATP. When ATP loses all of its phosphate, all that is left is adenosine (ATP is adenosine triphosphate), and the adenosine is only a purine (adenine) attached to a ribose. Therefore, fructose induces a massive degeneration of ATP, releasing large amounts of adenosine. This is eventually transformed into uric acid, the main plasma antioxidant, and we know that in excess it is not beneficial. Further, the small amount of vitamin C that is provided by fruit is outweighed by the increase in glycemia that it produces.

Finally, oxidative stress levels are determined by the antioxidant defense system, which consists of enzyme and non-enzyme systems, with enzyme systems being by far more important. Many of these enzymes require selenium (glutathione peroxidase), iron (catalase), zinc, copper, and manganese (superoxide dismutase), and given their similarity to toxic heavy metals, the heavy metal ions will compete to occupy the place in the enzyme, thereby inhibiting the enzyme's activity.

Non-enzymatic antioxidants have a limited effect, since they become neutralized when reacting with a free radical, unable to fight anymore.

133

Enzymatic antioxidants, on the other hand, can neutralize several free radicals. In order for enzyme systems to operate at full capacity, they need an adequate cellular concentration of selenium, zinc, and manganese, in which they are often deficient. Aside from the trace elements, the levels of glutathione are directly linked to the levels of cysteine. The enzymatic antioxidant systems are the first line of defense against free radicals; second are the non-enzymatic antioxidants, such as uric acid, antioxidant vitamins such as ascorbic acid (vitamin C), alpha-lipoic-acid (thioctic acid), retinol (vitamin A), tocopherol (vitamin E), carotene, bilirubin and plasma proteins.

**What are the consequences of excess oxidative stress?**

The list would be endless, since in every degenerative disorder there is an increase in the production of reactive species of oxygen and a decrease in the capacity of antioxidant defenses. Some of the most significant disorders are:

- Neurodegenerative diseases such as: Parkinson's, Alzheimer's, progressive supranuclear palsy, multiple sclerosis, schizophrenia, etc.
- Cancer.
- Premature aging.
- Deterioration of the skin, wrinkles.
- Lowered life expectancy.
- Reduced capacity for recovery in athletes after training.
- Atherosclerosis.
- Cataracts and retinopathy.
- Liver and kidney damage.
- Complications from diabetes.
- Infertility (the gonads are very sensitive to oxidative stress).
- Thyroid disorders (the reactive species of thiobarbituric acid resulting from lipid peroxidation play an important role).
- Immunosuppression and lower resistance to any type of external threat

# VARIZAPPER

The Zapper is a frequency generator invented by Dr. Clark to eliminate pathogens from the body. It emits a 9-volt electrical current at a frequency of 32,000 Hz. This frequency, when applied to our body with a sufficient voltage, kills off virtually every type of pathogen. While Dr. Clark must be credited with making the greatest contribution to promoting the use of the Zapper, the principles of its operation  were discovered and researched in the 1930s by Royal Raymond Rife. Rife stated that each species transmits a unique and characteristic frequency, and if any living being was radiated with its own frequency, it would grow weaker or die. In 2000, an engineer named Bob Beck wrote a book titled *Take Back Your Power*. He had designed a very simple electronic circuit to which the person connects themselves using two handles. The electric current travels through the body, destroying the pathogens living in it by "electrocuting" them. (Bob Beck was also a strong proponent of the use of colloidal silver).

Dr. Clark started her experimentation by determining the frequency of each pathogen to thus be able to examine what pathogens are living in each patient. After testing the patient and seeing what pathogens were present, she connected him or her to the frequency generator and destroyed the pathogens one by one, adjusting the frequency of the generator to each pathogen. Being that many different pathogens can usually be found in a patient, this method required the patient to be connected to the generator for hours in order to destroy all the pathogens. Also, this method required a person with the ability to test. This convinced Dr. Clark to continue looking into other options. A few years later she discovered that a positive output frequency of 32,000 Hz was effective at destroying all types of pathogens, which reduced the treatment time to one hour.

For more information on Dr. Hulda Clark visit www.drclark.net

The only limitation that the VariZapper has is that it cannot reach the interior of the eyeballs, bile ducts, digestive tract, bladder, tumors, abscesses, or severely poisoned organs.

Therefore, zapping must be complemented by parasite-purging, anti-bacterial, and anti-fungal supplements such as black walnut hull tincture, colloidal silver, etc.

On the other hand, this frequency generator has a number of beneficial effects that go far beyond its anti-pathogenic action. It **activates the immune system**, as it is a powerful immunostimulant that enhances phagocytosis, "energizing" our white blood cells even when they are poisoned with heavy metals, PCBs, benzene, asbestos, or dyes. It also **gives north polarity to organs**. Under ideal conditions, all organs, except for the brain, should have north polarity. When organs are ill, their polarity changes to south. This change in polarity favors the settlement of pathogens in the organ, but by polarizing the organ north, we create a hostile environment for pathogens and gradually help the organ regain its health and proper functioning. Thus, zapping should not be seen as an emergency measure, but rather as a great way to maintain health that will benefit everyone who does it on a daily basis.

To know whether a frequency generator is trustworthy, it has to be tested with an oscilloscope to verify that the current output is 100% positive; if not, it would be harmful. For this reason, we must avoid untested frequency generators. **The frequency generators used in Clark Therapy, known as VariZappers, conform to Dr. Clark's specifications and are completely safe and effective.**

The ideal is to use the frequency generator before 9:00 p.m., which is approximately when organs change their polarity from north to south to rest, though it can also be used after that time.

It is totally harmless, even for pets and babies under the age of 2 (taking into consideration that a classic parasite removal program should be done in both cases. Look at the programs on pages 61, 62, and 63).

The device should not be used by pregnant women or persons with a pacemaker, for the simple reason that its effect on that population has not been tested.

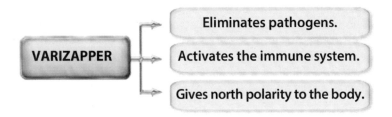

VARIZAPPER

- Eliminates pathogens.
- Activates the immune system.
- Gives north polarity to the body.

For more information on Dr. Hulda Clark visit www.drclark.net

## PROGRAMS FOR USE OF THE VARIZAPPER

- **"Standard zapping program": 7', 20', 7', 20', 7'** (7 minutes on, 20 minutes pause, 7 minutes on, 20 minutes pause, and 7 minutes on).
- **"Duration zapping": 60 continuous minutes** (this is the most common duration, but it can be applied for longer).

## THERE ARE SEVERAL OPTIONS TO CONNECT IT TO THE BODY:

- **Straps:** used for normal zapping and allow a large degree of freedom of movement. They are normally placed on the wrists, but if sensitive skin causes redness or a rash to appear, they can be placed on the forearms or ankles. However, the best way to prevent irritation is to wet the straps with colloidal silver.

- **Conductive slippers:** used for prolonged zapping procedures or if the wristbands produce irritation on sensitive skin.

- **Carbon cylinders:** They are used, like the conductive shoes, if the straps produce slight irritation on sensitive skin. The zapping is done while seated with your feet on the cylinders. They can also be held in the hands.

- **Body electrodes with Velcro fastening:** used to enhance the effect of the zapping in the urogenital and lower abdomen areas; they are attached at the upper thigh area or around the waist.

- **Gel electrodes:** used to focus the effect of the zapping and are normally placed on the lower abdomen area (although the zapping is unable to penetrate as much with these as it does with other systems).

**NOTE: THE VARIZAPPER DOES NOT NEGATIVELY AFFECT BACTERIAL INTESTINAL FLORA.**

141

## USING THE VARIZAPPER

1. First, select the most appropriate connection accessory to attach th VariZapper to your body. If you use straps, moisten them under water firs squeezing the yellow foam so that is fully soaked but not dripping.

2. Attach the straps to the wrists (or to the forearms or ankles if you have sensitive skin and redness appears on the wrists), with the yellow foam or the inside, i.e. in contact with the skin. Leave the connection buttons in the most comfortable area, and then put on the heads of the connection cable Tighten the straps to ensure good contact with the skin, so that the current can penetrate effectively, but without cutting off blood supply.

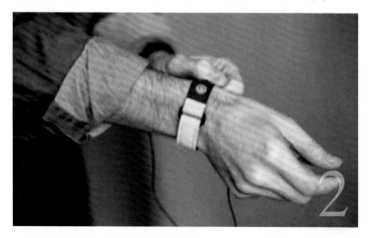

**3.** Connect the heads of the Zapper cable to the push buttons. It is not relevant which color goes on which side. Connect the other end of the cable to the VariZapper.

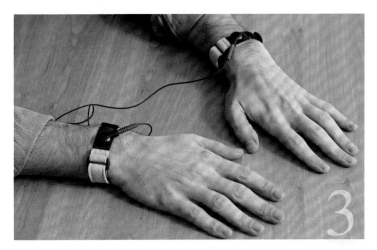

**4.** Turn on the VariZapper by pressing the "ON" button.

While using the VariZapper, it is recommended to not cross your arms or legs to achieve the best results. You might otherwise short circuit the current.

For more information on Dr. Hulda Clark visit www.drclark.net

**5.** Select the CONTINUOUS ZAP program, pressing the button marked with a dov arrow once and then the button in the center marked with an "S" for "start".

**6.** The 59:59 minutes remaining will appear on the screen and the zappir program takes its course. You only have to wait for the time to run out, which time the VariZapper will turn off automatically. Any activity can k done during this time. If you hear beeps during the zapping and th message *"no load"* appears on the screen, it means that the straps are n tight enough, the sponges are not wet enough, or the connectors are n making good contact with the connection buttons. You can interrupt th zapping whenever we want. Also, it is not mandatory to complete the ft 60 minute program – but you should never zap less than three times seve minutes over the course of an hour.

Steps 4, 5, and 6 are common to all connection accessories.

For more information on Dr. Hulda Clark visit www.drclark.net

**7.** If you use conductive slippers, remove the yellow foam inlays and wet them under water. Then connect the connection cable heads to the connection buttons on the on the slippers.

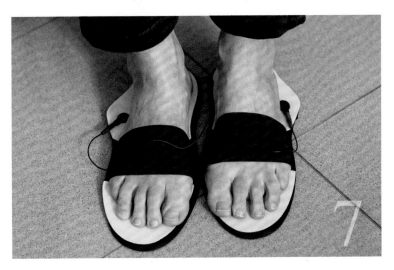

**8.** If you use the carbon cylinders, connect the connection cable to the cylinders and zap through the soles of your feet as shown in the picture.

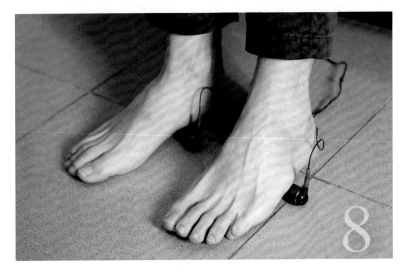

For more information on Dr. Hulda Clark visit www.drclark.net

**9.** If you use Velcro band electrodes, tighten them around your thighs poss to the groin. The larger bands can also be fastened around the abdomen

**10.** When using the gel electrodes, place them close to the area to be trea such that the current will flow through that area, without placing electro directly on damaged skin areas.

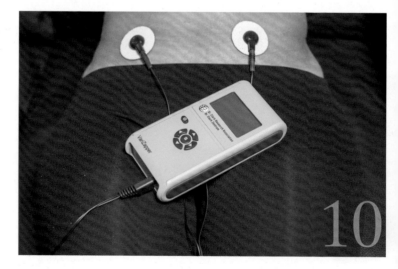

For more information on Dr. Hulda Clark visit www.drclark.net

# ZAPPLATES

When a specific organ has a dysfunction, infection, overload, etc., it is advisable to use, in addition to the VariZapper (which works on the entire body), the Zapplates on that specific organ for 20 minutes a day.

This is because when an organ has a problem, it is very likely that it is full of toxins. These toxins (especially PCBs) make it difficult for the current of the VariZapper to penetrate that organ. If, in this case, we apply "regular" zapping, we would not totally penetrate that organ because those toxins would cause an insulating effect and the frequencies sent by the VariZapper would not reach the interior of the affected organ. As Dr. Clark discovered, by zapping with plates, we reach all parts of the poisoned organ. The Zapplates are connected to the VariZapper to direct all of its vibrational power to a specific organ, tissue, or cell. We can also zap a specific pathogen throughout the body or in a specific organ or tissue, but as it is difficult to know all of the pathogens we are infected with (it would require a Syncrometer tester testing you), it is better to make a general sweep to exterminate them all.

Thanks to the zapping plates, we can also zap a localized pain, taking the frequency of the affected tissue or organ; or we can reinforce the action or regulate the production of any substance produced by the body (neurotransmitter, hormone, etc.) by zapping the secretory organ. But we will not explain these techniques in this text, as they are advanced techniques of Clark Therapy.

For more information on Dr. Hulda Clark visit www.drclark.net

## USING ZAPPLATES

1. The first step is to wet the straps. Connect the two red banana plugs of the special Plate Zapping Cable to the plates; then connect the push buttons of the wrist straps; and finally, connect the other end of the cable, which looks like a telephone connection, to the VariZapper (using the adapter to connect the cable to the VariZapper).

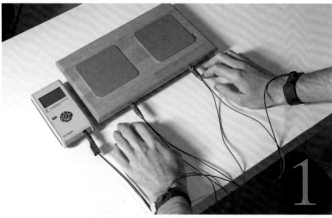

2. The next step is to put the frequency or frequencies to be zapped on the plates. These frequencies ("bottle copies", "specimens" or "samples") are available with all distributors of Clark products. First, we are going to zap an organ: for example, the pancreas. We will place the sample bottle of the pancreas on the right plate and the entire positive effect of zapping will go exclusively to that organ, although the connection is at the wrists like during regular zapping.

For more information on Dr. Hulda Clark visit www.drclark.net

**3.** If we want to zap a set of organs, such as the endometrium, the uterus, the cervix, and the fallopian tubes, we put the four frequency vials on the right plate without them touching each other. In this fashion, the benefits of zapping (elimination of pathogens, activation of the immune system and north polarization) will act on all four organs.

**4.** If we want to zap the white blood cells to activate the immune system, we put the white blood cell bottle on the right plate, by which we will be "energizing them" more than in a normal zapping.

For more information on Dr. Hulda Clark visit www.drclark.net

**5.** If we want to zap the blood of the brain, we put the bottle copy of the blood on the left plate and the one for the brain on the right plate. If you want to zap the blood of another organ, you would simply change the vial for the brain with the vial for another organ. This type of blood/organ zapping penetrates even deeper in to all the "crevices" of the organ and is usually done after zapping the organ.

**6.** If we want to zap a parasite like *Anisakis*, we put its bottle on the right plate. In this way, if this parasite were in our body, we would attack it. If it were not in our body, then the zapping would not have any effect on us (neither good nor bad).

**7.** If we want to zap a pathogen in an organ, we put the sample of the pathogen on the left plate and the sample of the organ on the right plate. Take, for example, *Eurytrema pancreaticum* in the pancreas. The zapping will act against this particular parasite in this particular organ only, which is why in general we think it is better to zap an organ without focusing on a pathogen, in order to attack all of the parasites that might be in that organ.

8. To start the zapping process, just as we did earlier, we turn on the VariZapper and choose the CONTINUOUS ZAP program, pressing the button marked with a down arrow once and then the button in the center marked with an "S". The 59:59 remaining will appear on the screen and we only have to wait for the time to run out, at which time the VariZapper will turn off automatically. If you hear beeps during the zapping and the message "no load" appears on the screen, it means that the straps are not tight enough, the sponges are not wet enough, or the connectors are not making good contact with the connection buttons.

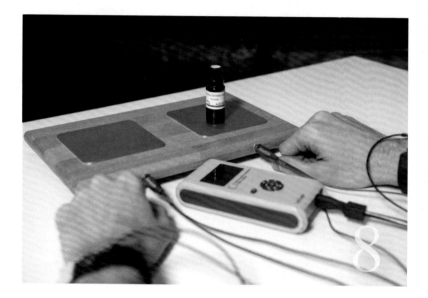

**IT IS IMPORTANT THAT THE SAMPLE BOTTLES NOT BE IN CONTACT WITH MAGNETS SINCE THEY WOULD LOSE THE FREQUENCY IMPRINTED ON THEM**

# FOOD ZAPPICATOR

The Zappicator has several functions, the first of which is to **energize** and vitalize: foods, water, cosmetics, drugs, supplements, etc.

Foods packed in any type of material (except metal) can be zapped, including precooked foods.

It is recommended to apply it to foods if you are not sure about the presence of pathogens (fish, meat, foods close to their expiration date, etc.) because it will eliminate several of them. It destroys eggs and different stages of parasites, bacteria, viruses, fungi, spores, and prions that can be found in dairy products, meat, and fish.

The second function is to provide north polarity to zapped foods, which is the same as making them "fresher." Recently picked vegetables and fruits have north polarity, but as the days pass this changes to south polarity. If they have been exposed to herbicides and pesticides, they are south polarized even when fresh. The same happens with water; when it runs through nature it has north polarity, but takes on south polarity when it stagnates or is packaged. As we have already seen, we have to consume food with north polarity in order to be healthy, since this is the healthy polarity for the human body.

Lastly, the Zappicator **neutralizes the toxins** contained in food, such as allergens, causing the food to become less allergenic. It also reduces the activity of benzene, azo dyes, and phenols contained in food, decreasing their absorption (it oxidizes benzene, transforming it into phenol); it destroys phloridzin, chlorogenic and gallic acids (substances naturally occurring in plants that Dr. Clark found to be harmful for certain groups of patients), changes the structure of PCBs to one that is less harmful, and changes the unnatural D-amino acids, such as D-phenylalanine and D-cysteine, into natural L-amino acids.

For more information on Dr. Hulda Clark visit www.drclark.net

## USING THE FOOD ZAPPICATOR

1. Put the foods, including any food packed in plastic containers or in any other materials (except metals) on the plate.

2. Connect the red end of the zapper cable to the Zappicator's push button and turn on the VariZapper. Choose the ZAPPICATOR program, pressing the button marked with a down arrow twice and then the button in the center marked with an "S" for "start".

**3.** The 9:59 minutes remaining will appear on the screen and we only have to wait for the time to run out, at which time the VariZapper will turn off automatically. Run this cycle twice before storing the food and before you prepare it.

Ozone is one of the most powerful oxidizing agents. Since the beginning of the 20th century, it has been used in the treatment of several diseases. There are clinics that treat a wide range of diseases using exclusively ozone. However, it is not necessary to use expensive, professional ozone generators.

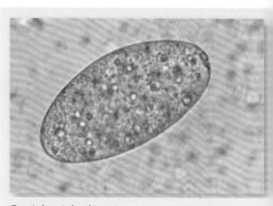

*Fasciolopsis buski egg*

There are domestic generators that can be used for the purpose of improving health. These devices allow you to ozonate foods, beverages, and rooms. For example, ozonating water and oil gives these liquids interesting detoxifying properties and helps to fight infections. Ozonated oil that is ingested exterminates the latent viruses in the cells and prevents a subsequent outbreak. It also exterminates tapeworms, *Ascaris*, parasite eggs, and Candida. Many bacteria also succumb to its effects.

The oil used for these purposes is extra virgin olive oil, since it is the ideal medium to transport ozone, which dissolves better in lipids than in aqueous solutions. When the oil is ozonated, it forms peroxides, hydroperoxides, ozonides, and aldehydes with a powerful germicide action. The ozonation lasts at most four days in oil, which means that it is recommended to consume the oil or apply it locally (for topical use) in the three days following ozonation. Also make sure to store it in the refrigerator. Never consume it with antioxidant supplements, since the ozone will oxidize them, thereby making them ineffective. The ozonated oil is effective precisely because it is a powerful oxidant.

The azo dyes and phenolic and estrogenic substances contained in food can be destroyed by ozonating it for 15 minutes. Clark Therapy recommends that people who are ill, and in general all immunosuppressed people, ozonate all of their food due to the disinfecting, non-poisoning, and highly penetrating effect of ozone. Cancer sufferers are highly toxic with cyanides, generally ingested through chlorinated water, and this toxicity inhibits the formation

For more information on Dr. Hulda Clark visit www.drclark.net

and correct functioning of many enzymes.

Put the food in a plastic bag, with the hose of the ozonator inside. Ozonate for 10 minutes, then wait another 10 minutes before opening the bag to allow the ozone to act.

By drinking a glass of water that has been ozonated for 5 minutes, and drinking it in less than 20 seconds (since ozone evaporates from water quickly, but not from oil), the level of cyanide drops considerably and the body is able to produce more energy and detoxify.

The benefit of ozone over other disinfectants is that, aside from how quickly it acts, when it is converted into oxygen it does not leave any toxic residue. We must remember that ozonation leaves a slight taste on the food. Ozonate your surroundings – office, house, meeting room, car, etc., any enclosed space – for 10 minutes to eliminate germs (parasites, mites, etc.).

**Important: do not ozonate a space when a person or pet is present.**

## USING THE OZONATOR

### Ozonating liquids (water, oil, etc.)

1. We first connect the ozonator to the electric current and make sure that the red POWER indication is lit. We then insert the silicone hose in the opening on the right front area.

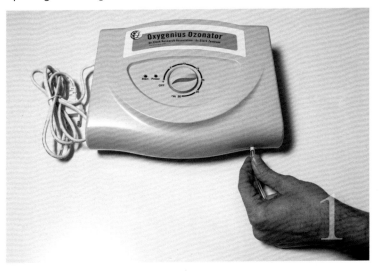

For more information on Dr. Hulda Clark visit www.drclark.net

**2.** You can use the diffusor rock so that the ozone exits more smoothly, since the bubbles formed are smaller and there is a lower risk that the liquid spurts out. Also, this increases the surface of the air that is blown through the oil or water and will improve the absorption of ozone into the oil or water.

**3.** Place the silicone hose with or without the diffusor in the container with the liquid to be ozonated.

For more information on Dr. Hulda Clark visit www.drclark.net

**4.** Turn the timer, which is in the OFF position, to the amount of time you wish to ozonate.

The effect of the ozonation lasts approximately 20 seconds in water and four days in oil, so it is recommended to ozonate only the amount that will be consumed within that time.

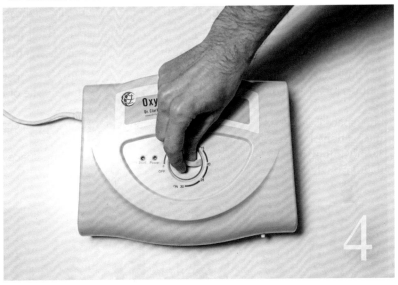

**3.** Connect the ozonator to the electrical current and turn the timer to 10 minutes. Once this period of time has elapsed, the ozonator will turn off. Let the food sit for another 10 minute to allow the ozone to act, then take the food out to eat.

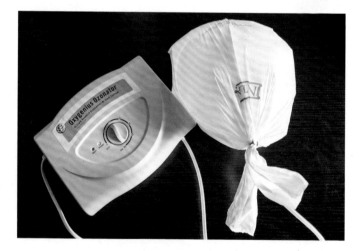

# WATER DISTILLER

In her book *The Cure and Prevention of All Cancers*, Dr. Clark states that the first and most important aspect for treatment in order to stop a degenerative process is to use water that contains no chlorine and none of the principal immunosuppressant agents.

Distilling is a simple and inexpensive process for obtaining water that is free of toxins that harm our health. Drinking and cooking with distilled water is essential for every person who is looking to maintain his or her health and above all for every person suffering from a degenerative illness.

## HANDLING THE WATER FILTER

1. Pour water in the bucket of the filter until it reaches the line with the word FULL.

For more information on Dr. Hulda Clark visit www.drclark.net

**2.** Put the carbon filter in its place. First, we put the tongue in place and ther introduce the other end until we hear a "click," which tells us that it i securely locked.

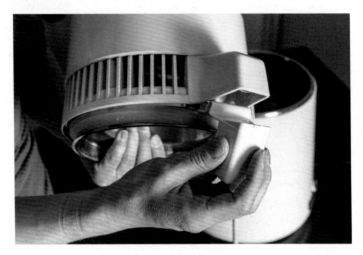

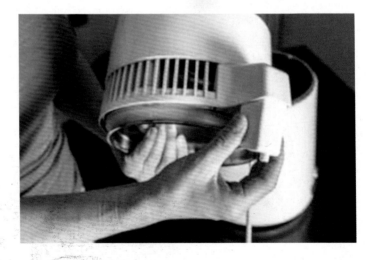

**3.** Place the top on the base of the distiller and connect the cable of the top to the socket on the base.

**4.** Place the glass pitcher under the water outlet located under the carbon filter. Connect the filter to the electrical current and push the start button.

The process takes 4 hours for every quart of water (maximum capacity of the device). You can also distill a lesser amount of water if you want, which then requires a shorter distilling time.

For more information on Dr. Hulda Clark visit www.drclark.net

# COLLOIDAL SILVER GENERATOR

Consuming colloidal silver is another effective method for fighting off pathogens. It is a colloid of very small silver particles that are suspended in pure water. Its greatest property is that it is capable of fighting 650 types of bacteria, thus preventing side effects of treatment with antibiotics. Prior to the discovery of antibiotics, in the first third of the 20th century (especially in the United States) colloidal silver was widely used to treat bacterial infections.

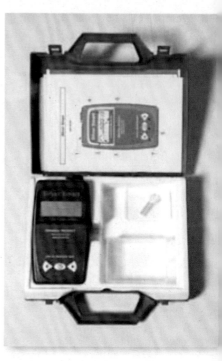

In 1920, Albert Searle, founder of the pharmaceutical company that bears his name, wrote a book titled *The Use of Colloids in Health and Disease*, which gained a wide following.

The anti-microbial virtues of silver had been known for many centuries, which perhaps explains why wealthy families used silver cutlery and dishes, and why a silver coin used to be placed in milk containers to delay its expiration.

However, with the arrival of sulfonamides and later antibiotics, colloidal silver was pushed further and further into the background. But this was not because silver was not as effective as the other two, but rather because it was more expensive to produce and, more than anything else, because it could not be patented.

When silver is in colloidal form, it does not interfere with the body's physiological processes, nor does it accumulate or form toxic deposits. Therefore, none of the side effects that happen when silver is ingested occur with colloidal silver. Substances in colloidal suspension have minimal toxic effects, even when ingested at levels greater than recommended.

Fish, for example, survive in water with an amount of lead six times greater than what is considered fatal if the metal is in colloidal form; however, in water with much lower concentrations of lead in non-colloidal form, they die quickly.

Colloidal silver is effective beginning with concentrations of 5 PPM (parts per million). We must be wary of those of high concentration and that are yellowish in color. We believe that it is best to purchase a colloidal silver generator and make it at home, because it is much less expensive and the quality is higher. Plus, we know the exact amount of parts per million that we need to make.

Colloidal silver only affects unicellular organisms such as protozoa, viruses, bacteria, and fungi; it does not affect human tissue, which is multicellular. It acts by blocking the oxygen intake of the microbe, causing it to suffocate. This statement might lead you to believe that colloidal silver is effective only for aerobic organisms (which require oxygen for metabolism), but it is also effective against many strains of anaerobic pathogens such as *Clostridium* bacteria, and against viruses which do not even have a metabolism. Its effective use as an anti-viral agent has also been demonstrated in laboratory settings. It seems that the mere contact of a silver particle with a virus renders the latter inactive, even if it does not have respiratory enzymes. However, what is surprising is that colloidal silver does not affect intestinal flora; to the contrary, it is very effective for gastrointestinal infections such as colitis, gastroenteritis, typhoid, dysentery, and cholera. This is probably because colloidal silver is absorbed easily and therefore does not reach the colon or even the lower parts of the small intestine. It is also very helpful that colloidal silver does not interact with any other treatment, be they allopathic or biological.

Robert Becker, one of the great proponents of colloidal silver, concluded after numerous observations that it is not only a powerful germicide, but **also promotes tissue regeneration, the healing of wounds,** and increased bone mass, especially in the elderly. He rightfully said that colloidal silver is like a second immune system.

However, there are false claims about the use of colloidal silver, for example that it can cause argyria. Argyria is a poisoning by silver compounds resulting in an intense blue coloration of the skin, but this only happens if silver salts are taken, not ionic or colloidal silver.

Let's look at how the effects of colloidal silver are entirely opposite of those caused by antibiotics:

For more information on Dr. Hulda Clark visit www.drclark.net

- Antibiotics cause weakness, while colloidal silver invigorates.
- Antibiotics make us sick, while colloidal silver heals us.
- Antibiotics weaken defenses, while colloidal silver strengthens them.
- Antibiotics are harmful, while colloidal silver is harmless.
- Antibiotics have a limited scope, while colloidal silver works on a broad spectrum.
- Antibiotics eliminate intestinal flora, encouraging the growth of fungi. In contrast, colloidal silver eliminates fungi, encouraging the growth of the intestinal flora.

## TIPS FOR MAKING HIGH-QUALITY COLLOIDAL SILVER

- The rods must be 999 parts per thousand silver, that is, of the highest purity.
- The rods must be completely clean, since they turn black after each use. To clean them, wipe them with a paper towel while they are still wet, and once they are dry, rub with a cloth as if to shine them.
- Do not use ozonated water.
- Water must be at room temperature.
- Keep all colloidal silver solution at room temperature.
- Use only distilled or reverse osmosis water when making colloidal silver, since high-quality colloidal silver solution must only contain silver and water; as we know, all other types of water contain toxins, which in addition may react with the silver particles.
- The concentration or parts per million (PPM) is not very important; it only needs to be at least 2.5 PPM. The size of the particles is much more important (the smaller the better), as is the amount of silver atoms that are in ionic state. When the concentration exceeds 20 PPM, the silver is no longer colorless and starts to turn yellow. This indicates that the particles are too large and thus the preparation will be less effective.
- The effective dose in infectious processes is 3 tablespoons per day, one before each meal, but it can be increased to 200 ml per day depending on the severity. This dose, though it may seem excessive, is completely harmless and should be used in cases where fast and decisive action is needed.
- It is advisable to start with maximum doses, lowering them as health is re-established.
- From what is said above, it is readily apparent how erroneous it is to use drops of colloidal silver, since they have concentrations of up to 200 PPM with large particles; they are therefore less effective, and the

dose is insufficient. Furthermore, for the same price as a couple of bottles of colloidal silver, we can buy a pair of silver rods and a generator that will allow us to make approximately 250 gallons of colloidal silver.

- Just 5 PPM destroys viruses and bacteria in 3-4 minutes.
- It is non-toxic.
- For external or internal use: skin cancer, eczema, acne, mosquito bites, etc.
- It can also be used on animals.
- It can be used as nose drops or eye drops.
- The generator makes between 10 PPM and 30 PPM. I recommend not going over 20 PPM and instead taking more of a 10 PPM solution, rather than going higher on the concentration.
- Normal dosage used as prevention: 1½ teaspoons 2-3 times a day.
- For mouthwash: ½-1 teaspoon with a little bit of water for approximately 3 minutes.
- Genital washes (fungi, etc.)
- Helps in the scarring of wounds.

## USING THE COLLOIDAL SILVER GENERATOR

**1.** First, place the batteries in the rear compartment and then the two silver rods in the sockets intended for them.

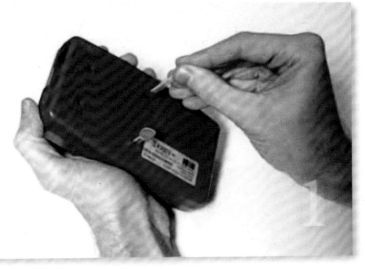

For more information on Dr. Hulda Clark visit www.drclark.net

**2.** Pour distilled water in the plastic container that comes with the generator, up to the marked line.

**3.** Place the generator on the plastic container filled with distilled water, with the rods in the water.

For more information on Dr. Hulda Clark visit www.drclark.net

Turn the silver generator on with the center button and push the buttons marked with arrows to the right and left to adjust the concentration at which the generator will make the colloidal silver, for example at 15 PPM. After a while it will have finished process, and we will have colloidal silver of the highest quality. The duration of the process depends on the purity of the water that you use – the purer the water, the longer the process of electrolysis takes. Using highly purified water, it is not unusual for the process to take more than an hour.

# FULL SPECTRUM LIGHT

Ancient civilizations were aware of the myriad of effects that sunlight has on health. Hippocrates and Pythagoras wrote about its benefits.

Heliotherapy treated physical and mental pathologies with sunlight hundreds of years ago. It is the scientific precursor to the therapeutic use of full spectrum light. Herodotus, the father of heliotherapy, wrote that daily exposure to the full spectrum of the sun is necessary for the prevention of illness. Niels Finsen (Nobel Prize in Physiology in 1903) used full spectrum light to treat lupus and Alzheimer's.

Many other scientists have also used it successfully in the treatment of Parkinson's and auto-immune disorders.

Now, years later, we have a comfortable solution to help us: the "full spectrum light box" for indoor spaces. Using for just an hour and a half per day gives us all of the benefits that this "blue-white" light has to offer.

## How does full spectrum light work?

Full spectrum light enters through the eyes and the photoreceptors of the skin, reaching the hypothalamus (known as the "brain of the brain"), which controls part of the nervous system and regulates most of the body's metabolic processes.

The hypothalamus controls body temperature, hunger, thirst, blood pressure, and, according to Dr. Clark, stops the onset of tumors and links our nervous system with our endocrine system. It also runs our "master gland," the pituitary gland, which secretes essential hormones.

The hypothalamus regulates our stress level, affects our emotions, and controls our immune functions. Likewise, our body clock is located in the hypothalamus and controls our circadian (daily) rhythms, but to do this it needs adequate light followed by darkness. Therefore, the inadequate lighting we are subject to on a daily basis has a negative impact on our health, since our hypothalamic body clock is connected to the pineal gland. This gland secretes the important hormone melatonin, which is essential for proper sleep.

In addition, serotonin, which is related to our mood, is increased with exposure to full-spectrum light and drops if we do not have access to it (for example, if we receive indoor lighting for most of the day). Also, the production of sex hormones (testosterone, FSH, and estradiol) is regulated by exposure to this light.

It has been scientifically proven that conventional indoor lighting can cause headaches, stress, and eye and muscle fatigue, as well as hormonal imbalances in men and women (irregular menstruation, impotence, etc.)
Companies that use full-spectrum lighting have higher performance and productivity in the workplace, a lower level of absenteeism, and better employee health. Schools that use this lighting note a higher level of learning in their students and a lower level of stress.
A study conducted in 1980 shows that conventional indoor lighting increases the levels of the stress hormones ACTH and cortisol, which produces mental agitation, fatigue, irritability, hyperactivity, and attention and learning problems in children and adults.
Dr. Laurence Martel, president of the National Academy of Integrative Learning, affirms that full-spectrum lighting is a key element for improving learning and health, comparing the effects of bad lighting to those of poor nutrition. An article published in *the journal Environmental Health Perspectives* states that inadequate lighting is one of the greatest dangers to children and adults and supports the use of full-spectrum lighting in schools and workplaces.
All of us would need, in order to achieve proper physical and mental health, at least an hour and a half of full-spectrum light per day.
It is practically impossible to achieve this in today's world, not only because of cloudy or rainy days when the light we receive is "poor," but also because of the pollution that covers our cities, preventing the full spectrum of light from reaching us even in the summer.
Also, we spend most of our days indoors with inadequate and unhealthy conventional lighting. Windows and sunglasses filter out part of the wavelengths present in the full-spectrum sunlight.
We also have to consider that children and the elderly spend hours a day in classrooms and other rooms that lack healthy lighting, with all of the negative effects on health that this leads to.

Now we can have all of the benefits of full-spectrum light indoors, with no negative side effects.
Since we cannot force schools and workplaces to use full-spectrum lighting, it

173

is important that we use the "full-spectrum light box" at home for at least one hour and a half.

Our plants and animals also benefit from full-spectrum light since it improves mood, health, and growth in our pets and reduces the maintenance of plants.

## Full-spectrum light and Clark Therapy

Dr. Clark successfully used full-spectrum light in her therapy for years.

Her studies describe the benefits of full-spectrum light and emphasize the benefits of exposure to this light for everyone, as it can be used to prevent and treat minor, severe, and even auto-immune illnesses.

Her studies highlighted the following benefits of full-spectrum light:

— Increase in the activity of the immune system in the area treated: liver, breast, lungs, genitals, etc. White blood cells are activated, multiplying their ability to "devour" pathogens and toxins in the area where the light is applied. This happens because it eliminates the ferritin coating that usually covers and disables the white blood cells of sick people.

— Kills parasites (including liver flukes) and other pathogens in the areas where it is applied 4 to 8 inches from the body.

— Helps to regulate the production of pyruvic aldehyde and thiourea in cancer patients, which in these patients is derailed and, according to Dr. Clark, is what causes tumor growth.

— Neon light (including energy-efficient lamps), that we are exposed to for hours on end, promotes the production of thiourea, which increases abnormal cell division. This is why Dr. Clark recommends the application of full-spectrum light for tumors and other abnormal growths, in addition to improving health in general.

— Destroys parasite eggs, bacteria, and fungi in food, and disables the toxicity of azo dyes in them (after only 10 minutes of exposure).

— Improves sexual function, and digestion.

— Increases energy.

— Reduces eye fatigue caused by computer monitors, reading, etc.

— Lowers incidence of depression and increases good mood.

— Increases capacity for learning, concentration, and productivity.

— Reduces symptoms of chronic fatigue.

— Improves nighttime sleep.

— Accelerates recovery from jet lag.

**Why use the Dr. Clark "Full-Spectrum Light Box?"**

According to Dr. Clark's studies, in order for a full-spectrum light box to be truly effective, it has to have between 130 W and 140 W and a specific color temperature. Not all full-spectrum lights are equal, but the Dr. Clark "Full-Spectrum Light Box" meets all of these requirements.

**USING THE DR. CLARK FULL-SPECTRUM LIGHT BOX**

The Dr. Clark full-spectrum light box can be used in two ways:

**1. As general room lighting.**

2. For treatment, by placing it about 6 inches from the area to be treated.

For more information on Dr. Hulda Clark visit www.drclark.net

Or by placing it right on the area of the body to be treated (more effective for fighting pathogens and activating the immune system).

# FREQUENTLY ASKED QUESTIONS FROM PATIENTS ABOUT CLARK THERAPY

For more information on Dr. Hulda Clark visit www.drclark.net

**1. I have candidiasis, what can I do?**

The Bowel Cleanse is very effective as it uses anti-parasitic, anti-bacterial, and anti-fungal agents. To attack candidiasis we have to use more than just anti-fungals, since Candida always work in conjunction with parasites and bacteria.

However, we recommend the following protocol for cases of recurrent candidiasis:

- **1st** Do for 6 weeks (it is beneficial that your partner do it as well):
  — Black walnut hull tincture: for the first 6 days, take one tablespoon in a glass of cold water 15 minutes before breakfast. Drink it slowly. Once the bottle is open, store it in the refrigerator. On the 7th day: 3 tablespoons in a glass of cold water, also 15 minutes before breakfast. After: 3 tablespoons, once a week.
  — Turmeric: 3 with breakfast, lunch, and dinner.
  — Fennel: 3 with breakfast, lunch, and dinner.
  — Lugol's iodine (do not take if you are allergic to iodine): 6 drops in water, 4 times a day between meals.
  — Oregano oil: 5 drops in an empty capsule with 2 meals (take with a full stomach).
  — Vitamin C: 1 with breakfast, lunch, and dinner.
  — Vitamin B complex: 1 with breakfast.
  — Echinacea: 1 with breakfast and lunch.
  — Betaine: 1 with breakfast, lunch, and dinner.
  — Pau d'Arco: 2 with breakfast, lunch, and dinner.
  — Psyllium seeds: 1 tablespoon dissolved in a glass of water, both when you wake up and before you go to bed.
  — Garlic extract: 2 with breakfast, lunch, and dinner.
- **2nd** Kidney cleanse + once a week (all 3 supplements on the same day):
  — 3 tablespoons of black walnut hull tincture in a glass of water. Drink slowly for 15 minutes before a meal, wait another 15 minutes before eating food.
  — Once open, store in the refrigerator.
  — Lugol's iodine (do not take if you are allergic to iodine): 6 drops in

water, 4 times a day.
Take on the same day as the black walnut hull tincture.

— Oregano oil: 5 drops in an empty capsule with a meal (on a full stomach).

■ **3rd** Two or three liver cleanses (once every two weeks) + detoxification program for heavy metals and other toxins.

Note: the 2nd and 3rd programs each contain two protocols that have to be done simultaneously.

2. **Is it true that my levels of bad cholesterol will decrease if I cleanse my liver?**

Cholesterol levels normalize after doing several Liver Cleanses, since high levels usually result from an overloaded liver.

3. **What can I use to fight viruses?**

The VariZapper is effective, as are colloidal silver and Boswellia.

4. **What is the first organ cleanse that I should do?**

The Bowel Cleanse, since in order to do a proper organ detoxification, the first organ that has to be detoxified and free of pathogens is the intestine.

5. **Is it advisable for my partner to also do the Bowel Cleanse or the Parasite Program?**

Yes, it is advisable. Even though our partners may not show any symptoms, the most common situation is that many of the pathogens that one person has are also present in their partner, even if they do not engage in sexual intercourse.

6. **Why is oregano oil included in the bowel and kidney cleanses?**

To increase the effectiveness of the cleanses, given oregano oil's action against bacteria and fungi.

7. **Do I always have to do the maintenance Parasite Program?**

Yes, we recommend it because we are always exposed to pathogens in foods, restaurants, relationships, etc.

For more information on Dr. Hulda Clark visit www.drclark.net

**8. Why is it advisable to do a parasite removal of Ascaris every three or four months?**

Because it is a parasite that is very common and very prone to reinfection; its eggs can even be in the air that we breathe, and black walnut hull tincture does not kill them.

**9. Can I do a Liver Cleanse without doing a Parasite Cleanse or Bowel Cleanse beforehand?**

We recommend to first do a Bowel Cleanse, in particular to eliminate any pathogens that may be in our intrahepatic ducts. Furthermore, when the intestines are clean, the liver's "waste" will be eliminated more easily.

**10. Are the herbs for the liver the same as those for the Liver Cleanse?**

No, the Cleanse is a protocol for eliminating waste and stones, while the herbs only help to improve the liver's functioning without eliminating its waste.

**11. Can Liver Cleanses help with weight loss?**

Yes, because metabolism improves, as does digestion.

**12. Are Clark cleanses recommended for elite athletes?**

Yes, they are highly recommended, since they improve the absorption of nutrients, oxygenation, recovery, etc.

**13. I want to get pregnant, is it good for me to do organ cleanses?**

Yes, since several pathogens and toxins that the mother may have are usually passed on to the fetus; therefore, in our opinion it is essential to do them before becoming pregnant.

**14. Can I take immune system supplements at all times?**

Of course. Plus, these are also recommended to stimulate and feed our white blood cells.

**15. As a source of vitamin C, what is better to take: ascorbic acid or rose hips?**

It depends on the issue we are looking to address.

We will normally take vitamin C in capsules, but in the immune system support program we will take rose hips, since they are a strong antioxidant of selenium and germanium (which we will also take in this protocol). On the other hand, when taking large amounts (several grams per dose), taking only rose hips could cause constipation. Vitamin C capsules (ascorbic acid) do not cause this problem.

### 16. Why does oregano oil have to be taken in capsules?

Because it can irritate the oral or esophageal mucus membranes. The gastric mucus membranes, on the other hand, are prepared to withstand high degrees of acidity.

### 17. Why does HCL have to be taken in capsules?

For the same reason as oregano oil.

### 18. Capsules with HCL dissolve in seconds, can HCL harm the stomach?

No, the mucus of the stomach is prepared to withstand a highly acidic pH; furthermore, the HCL supplement is diluted to 5%.

### 19. Since it contains iodine, can Lugol's iodine affect my thyroid?

Only if the dosage were more than 30 drops per dose would iodine reach the thyroid gland, and even then, this is not to say that it would damage it. Using the normal dose of 6 drops will never affect the thyroid gland; its effect will be limited to the digestive system.

### 20. Is taking black walnut hull tincture the same as taking black walnut capsules?

No, the tincture is more effective.

### 21. Why are the containers of black walnut hull tincture so small?

Because once they are opened, even if they are kept refrigerated, the tincture loses its disease-fighting effectiveness within a few weeks.

### 22. Can consuming colloidal silver be harmful?

No, it does not cause toxicity in any case.

### 23. Is it bad to take so many vitamins?

No, water soluble vitamins are eliminated in urine. In order for fat soluble vitamins (A, D, E, and K) to cause toxicity, they have to be consumed in massive doses. Only vitamin D, taken in very high dosages, will usually cause problems. Pregnant women should not exceed 10,000 IU of vitamin A per day from all sources.

### 24. Can Lugol's iodine be taken if I have hyper- or hypothyroidism?

Yes, but you will need to consult your physician or therapist first.

### 25. Can any Clark supplement lead to a positive result in a drug test?

No.

### 26. Is it true that IP6 can improve my stamina in sports?

Yes, because it can increase cellular oxygenation to a significant degree.

### 27. Is it true that phytic acid (IP6) takes minerals away from the body?

No, it is not. IP6 is a chelator of heavy metals that serve no other purpose than to poison our bodies. It never steals minerals, since these minerals are part of our tissues. It needs to be consumed between meals, however, because just as it "catches" metals and radioactivity, it can do the same with the minerals contained in foods.

### 28. Can I zap my children or pets?

Of course, in fact we recommend it.

### 29. Which program do I use for the VariZapper: the 7, 20, 7, 20, 7 minute program, or the continuous program of 60 minutes?

It is more beneficial to use the continuous 60 minute program even if you have to stop it before the end of the cycle due to time constraints, because this way the beneficial action of the VariZapper (the removal of pathogens and the stimulation of the immune system) lasts for as long as you use it. This is not the case with the other program that acts for 7 minutes, then stops for 20 minutes, etc.

185

### 30. How many hours per day can I zap?

As long as you want; the longer the better. You can use the VariZapper several times a day for 10, 20, or 30 minutes or more, and for several hours in a row. Once the protocols are completed, it is advisable to continue using the VariZapper, even if it is only for only 20 minutes each day.

### 31. What can I do if the VariZapper's yellow straps irritate my skin?

People with sensitive skin can wet the straps with colloidal silver instead of water, or use carbon cylinders (on their feet), the conductive slippers, or the gel electrodes to solve this problem.

### 32. Can it be harmful to zap myself a lot?

On the contrary, zapping is beneficial since it eliminates the body's pathogens, provides north polarity to the organs, and activates the immune system by energizing the white blood cells.

### 33. Does the VariZapper kill the good bacteria of the intestine?

No, it does not affect the probiotic flora of the intestine.

### 34. Can I zap myself while I am eating?

Yes.

### 35. Which is better to put on first, the VariZapper or the Zapplates?

If you need to use both, the order is not that important, but the effectiveness may be greater by starting with the plates.

### 36. What is the difference between the VariZapper and the Zapplates?

The VariZapper acts on the whole body, while the Zapplates act only on the organ or organs that we choose. In this way, all the beneficial effects of zapping focus on that organ or those organs only, with the effect being more powerful on the selected organs since it does not act on the rest of the body. On the other hand, when we put the frequency of one or several pathogens on the zapping plates, we will only act against that or those pathogen(s). In doing so, we focus all of its power exclusively on the chosen pathogens and none on the rest of the pathogens we might have.

### 37. Is it bad to zap at night?

No, not at all. The only issue is that at night organs change their polarity to south to rest and when we zap we are "waking them from their rest." Nevertheless, it is preferable to zap at night than to not zap at all, if you have no other time available.

### 38. Do I have to wait for any specific period of time between zappings?

When zapping with plates, 10 minutes between each organ that is zapped.

### 39. Does zapping with adhesive electrodes have the same effectiveness as the carbon cylinders or straps?

To work on specific areas, yes, because the maximum effectiveness occurs in the area where they are placed; however, its effectiveness on the rest of the body is lower.

### 40. Can I zap if I am pregnant?

It is not recommended.

### 41. Can I use the zapping plates to zap one of my pet's organs?

Yes, it can be used in the same way as with a human, that is, by zapping the liver, kidney, etc.

### 42. Can biological fruit and vegetables be zapped?

Even if we collect them ourselves and know that they are fresh and do not contain any chemical fertilizers, it is always best to zap them because they may contain pathogens and toxins that are in the soil. Also, zapping is always positive since it provides north polarity, eliminates pathogens, and neutralizes toxins in food.

### 43. Can I zap food that is already cooked?

Yes, you should ideally zap food just before eating it.

### 44. Can I ozonate a room while I am inside it?

It is recommend that no person or animal be inside an enclosed space when you ozonate it. In the event of ozone inhalation, all that happens is a slight dryness in the respiratory system, since ozone is oxidizing. In order

187

for this to be dangerous, we would have to inhale a large amount of ozone.

## 45. Can I ozonate food that is already cooked?

Yes, of course.

## 46. How many times should I ozonate a room per week?

Once per week is enough.

## 47. Can colloidal silver be taken preventively on a continuous basis?

Yes, there is no problem in taking the equivalent of one teaspoon several times a day as a preventive measure.

## 48. How often does the filter of the distiller need to be replaced?

Every two months.

## 49. Is it better to use the full-spectrum light pressed against my stomach or 4 to 8 inches away from my body to help me with a liver disease?

The closer to the body, the better. It is also more comfortable because we can sit or lie down while holding it in the area.

## 50. Can the light box be worn with clothes?

To light up a room, yes, because we capture its benefits through our eyes' photoreceptors. For local applications, the light must be directly on the skin of the area to be treated.

## 51. How much time per day can I use the light box?

For in-room use, as long as you want until 9:00 or 10:00 p.m. For local application, as many times as you want, with the normal application ranging from 10 to 20 minutes each.

## 52. Can animals use the light box?

Yes, in the same way as humans.

### 53. Can any dentist remove amalgam fillings?

Yes, but it is preferable to inform them regarding the materials or trademarks that he or she must use as replacements; being that a "normal" dentist does not know which ones are non-toxic.

### 54. You warn not to take Lugol's iodine if I am allergic to iodine. How can I know whether I can take it?

Throughout our careers, neither Dr. Clark nor I have found any person who is allergic to Lugol's iodine. However, to test it, all you have to do is place a drop on the back of your hand and wait for a couple of minutes; if there is no allergic reaction, reddening, burning, etc., then there should not be any problem. In any case, this is just our opinion. If you have any doubts, consult your physician.

Any doubts or questions that you may have about the therapy or the protocols can be sent to customerservice@drclark.com, or ask any authorized Clark therapist.

# CLARK THERAPY PRODUCT GUIDE

- Amino acid complex
- Arginine
- Aspartic acid
- Betaine hydrochloride
- Birch bark tea
- Black cherry
- Black walnut hull (tincture and capsules)
- Boswellia
- Bromelain
- Calcium citrate
- Cascara sagrada
- Cayenne pepper
- Chromium
- Cloves
- Coenzyme Q10 (30 mg and 400 mg)
- Cysteine
- Digestive enzymes
- Echinacea
- Empty gelatin caps
- Epsom salt (capsules and powder)
- Eucalyptus
- Fennel
- Fenuthyme (thyme and fenugreek)
- Folic acid (vitamin B9)
- Garlic odorless extract
- Ginger (root)
- Ginkgo biloba extract
- Ginseng, Korean (extract)
- Glutamic acid
- Glutamine
- Glutathione
- Goldenrod tincture
- Green tea (extract)
- HCl (hydrochloric acid)
- Hydrangea (root)
- Inositol
- IP6 (inositol hexaphosphate or phytic acid)
- Iron (ferrous gluconate)
- Kidney Herbs

# CLARK THERAPY PRODUCT GUIDE

- Lipase & Pancreatin
- Liver Herbs
- Lugol's iodine (iodine solution)
- Lysine (capsules and powder)
- Magnesium oxide
- Manganese
- Methionine
- Mint oil
- MSM
- Multivitamin
- Nutmeg oil
- Omega 3
- Oregano oil
- Ornithine
- Papain
- Pau d'Arco (Tabebuia impetiginosa)
- Pepsin
- Potassium citrate
- Quassia
- Quercetin
- Reishi mushroom
- Rose hips
- Saw palmetto extract
- Selenium
- Slippery elm
- Sodium alginate
- Sodium bicarbonate
- St. John's Wort (Hypericum)
- Taurine
- Thioctic acid (alpha-lipoic-acid)
- Turmeric
- Tryptophan
- Uva ursi
- Valerian root extract
- Vitamin A (retinol)
- Vitamin B complex
- Vitamin B1 (thiamine)
- Vitamin B2 (capsules or powder)

191

- Vitamin B3 (niacin)
- Vitamin B3 (niacinamide)
- Vitamin B5 (pantothenic acid)
- Vitamin B6 (pyridoxine)
- Vitamin B7 (biotin)
- Vitamin B12 (cobalamine)
- Vitamin C (ascorbic acid) (capsules and powder)
- Vitamin C (ascorbic acid) (buffered)
- Vitamin D (cholecalciferol)
- Vitamin E (tocopherol)
- Wormwood
- Zinc gluconate

### ■ AMINO ACID COMPLEX:

Applications:

— Protein deficiency.
— Immune deficiencies.

Dosage:

— 2-5 capsules with each meal.

### ■ ARGININE:

Properties:

— Recommended by Dr. Clark for more energy through the day, especially when cutting back on coffee.
— Accelerates the scarring of wounds.
— Improves erectile response and sperm production and motility.
— Liver detoxicant.
— Increases the response of the immune system.
— Increases the production of collagen and muscle mass and reduces deposits of body fat.
— Reduces muscle spasms.
— Effective against hemorrhoids.
— Prevents the formation of atherosclerosis.
— Its deficiency can cause hair loss, constipation, and fatty liver.

Dosage:

— 2-6 capsules per day, 20 minutes before meals.

## ■ ASPARTIC ACID:

Properties:

— Liver protector and detoxicant.
— Boosts the immune system, increasing immunoglobulins and antibodies.
— Helps to eliminate ammonia from the body.
— Increases resistance to fatigue.

Indications:

— Chronic fatigue.
— Infections.
— Overloaded liver.

Dosage:

— 5 g, 15 minutes before 2 meals.

## ■ BETAINE HYDROCHLORIDE:

Properties:

— Eliminates fat from the liver.
— Helps with the digestion of proteins in the stomach.
— Helps with the absorption of iron and calcium.
— Increases acidity of the gastric environment.
— Provokes the secretion of pepsin.
— Improves the absorption of vitamins B and C.
— Helps with the sterilization of ingested food.
— Prevents the absorption of intestinal parasites.
— Helps to detoxify malonic acid from the kidneys.
— Eliminates Clostridium bacteria from the intestines.

Dosage:

— 1-2 capsules with each meal.

193

■ **BIRCH BARK TEA:**

Properties:

— Analgesic.
— Anti-inflammatory.
— Antiseptic.
— Scars wounds.
— Astringent and choleretic.

Indications:

— Urinary disorders.
— Gout.
— Obesity.
— Fever.
— Bile dysfunctions.
— Rheumatism.
— Helps to eliminate prions in degenerative patients.

Dosage:

— Make an infusion with about one ounce of herb per quart of water. Drink 3 glasses a day.

■ **BLACK CHERRY (CONCENTRATE):**

Properties:

— Diuretic.
— Kidney detoxicant.
— Analgesic.
— Anti-rheumatic.
— Reduces fever.

Indications:

— Part of the Kidney Cleanse.

■ **BLACK WALNUT HULL TINCTURE AND CAPSULES (Juglans nigra):**

Properties:

— Treatment against parasites, bacteria, viruses, and fungi.
— Improves bowel movements.
— Liver detoxicant.

Indications:

— Use as directed as part of the Parasite Program.
— External application for skin fungus.

## ■ BOSWELLIA:

Properties:

— Anti-viral.
— Anti-bacterial.
— Natural anti-inflammatory.

Indications:

— After surgical procedures.
— Inflammatory processes.
— Arthritis/osteoarthritis.
— Viral and bacterial processes.

Dosage:

— 2-6 capsules per day with meals.

## ■ BROMELAIN:

Properties:

— Anti-inflammatory.
— Digestive.

Dosage:

— Take one hour before breakfast, lunch, and/or dinner.
— Anti-inflammatory effect: 4-5 capsules.
— Digestive effect: 1 capsule with each meal.

## ■ CALCIUM (CITRATE):

Properties:

— Strengthens the bone system.
— Promotes sleep.
— Regulates coagulation processes.
— Promotes cardiovascular health.
— Helps in absorbing vitamin B12.

195

Indications:

— Osteoporosis.
— Irritability.
— Insomnia.
— Anemia.
— Allergies (reduces the levels of histamine).

Dosage:

— 2 capsules with 2 or 3 meals.

## ■ CASCARA SAGRADA:

Properties:

— Improves digestion.
— Cleans the colon.
— Increases appetite.
— Detoxifies the body.
— Facilitates bowel movements (stimulant laxative).

Indications:

— Problems with occasional constipation.
— Bowel Cleanse.

Dosage:

— 1 capsule per day with a main meal.

Contraindications:

— Do not take for longer than 3 weeks at a time. Do not take when you already have loose stool. Do not take when pregnant.

## ■ CAYENNE PEPPER:

Properties:

— Stimulates appetite and the secretion of gastric juices, thus increasing intestinal motility.
— Helps with circulation (especially microcirculation).

Indications:

— Anorexia.
— Hypochlorhydria (too little hydrochloric acid in the stomach).

— Bloating.
— Circulatory disorders.

Dosage:

— 1 capsule with each meal.

## ■ CHROMIUM:

Properties:

— Helps metabolize glucose and regulate blood sugar levels.
— Prevents the formation of atheromas.
— Promotes growth.
— Controls cholesterol levels.
— Stimulates the transport of amino acids and the synthesis of proteins.

Indications:

— Heart problems.
— Circulatory problems.
— Atherosclerosis.
— High cholesterol.
— Reduction in sperm formation.
— Hypoglycemia.
— Nervousness, irritability, depression.
— Type I and Type II Diabetes

Dosage:

— 1-2 capsules per day with meals.

## ■ CLOVES:

Properties:

— Antiseptic.
— Anti-bacterial.
— Anti-fungal.
— Carminative (stimulates gastric motility).
— Digestion and appetite stimulant.
— Attacks parasite eggs.
— Antioxidant.

197

# CLARK THERAPY PRODUCT GUIDE

Indications:

— Part of the Parasite Program.

Dosage:

— Up to 9 capsules per day.

■ **CO-ENZYME Q10 (30 mg and 400 mg):**

Properties:

— Increases the effectiveness of the immune system.
— At high doses it is an excellent parasite removal agent for roundworms (see *Ascaris* Parasite Program).
— Essential for the heart and brain: Improves the performance of both.
— Helps normalize blood pressure.
— Helps different enzymes in their function.
— Facilitates weight loss.
— Prevents aging.
— Relieves fatigue.
— Helps to improve tolerance of physical exercise.
— Promotes cellular oxygenation.
— Helps to maintain adequate levels of blood glucose.
— Carrier of electrons in cellular mitochondria, necessary in preventing degeneration.
— The most effective supplement against *Ascaris* in the brain, bone marrow, etc.

Indications:

— Diabetes (stimulates the synthesis and secretion of insulin).
— Periodontal Disease.
— Chronic fatigue syndrome.

Dosage:

— 1-3 capsules with each meal (30 mg), 1 capsule per day (400 mg) or take as indicated on the Ascaris Parasite Program.

■ **CYSTEINE:**

Properties:

— Helps to eliminate heavy metals from the body.

For more information on Dr. Hulda Clark visit www.drclark.net

— Helps in the excretion of mucus.
— Regulates enzyme activity.
— Immune system stimulant.
— Helps to detoxify malonic acid from the kidneys.
— Removes larvae and eggs from Ascaris and pinworm parasites.

Indications:

— Organ detoxification programs.
— Stimulation of the immune system.
— Fragile hair and nails.
— Eczema and psoriasis.
— Supports kidney function.
— Protects from the toxic effects of radiation.
— An antioxidant, quenches free radicals.
— Can be converted into glucose, and is therefore a source of energy.
— Helps in absorbing iron.
— Must be used with care by people who are highly acidic and diabetics (because it can lower the efficiency of insulin).
— It should ideally be taken 5 hours apart from taking ozonated olive oil or Lugol's iodine (because these are oxidants).

Dosage:

— 1-6 capsules per day with meals.

## ■ DIGESTIVE ENZYMES:

Properties:

— Facilitate the digestion of fats, proteins, and carbohydrates.
— Prevent the formation of intestinal gases due to the fermentation of undigested food.
— Inhibit certain allergenic substances that are ingested through food.
— Prevent inflammation and hypertrophy of the various organs that comprise the digestive system, above all the liver, the pancreas, and the gallbladder.
— Help bodily cleans and detoxification processes.
— Help to reduce pain and inflammation of wounds and traumas, thereby accelerating healing.
— Digest the remains of the exterminated parasites.

Dosage:

— 2-4 capsules with each meal.

■ **ECHINACEA:**

Properties:

— Activates the formation of leukocytes, stimulating the immune system.
— Anti-bacterial action.
— Anti-inflammatory.
— Digestive.
— Stimulates the secretion of saliva.

Indications:

— Pharyngitis, rhinitis, sinusitis, and bronchitis.
— Common flu and cold.
— Recurrent diarrhea and colitis; ulcerative stomatitis.
— Any type of infection.

Dosage:

— 4 capsules at breakfast, lunch, and dinner.

■ **EMPTY GELATIN CAPSULES:**

Indications:

— To encapsulate drops of oregano oil (or any other supplement that needs to be put into a capsule).

■ **EPSOM SALTS:**

Properties:

— Laxative.
— Facilitates the elimination of toxins.
— Helps to prevent migraines.
— Contains magnesium

Dosage:

— In capsules: 1-3 per day, 20 minutes before meals.
— In powder: 1 teaspoon per day.
— In liver cleanses: 15 capsules or 1 tablespoon for each dose.

# CLARK THERAPY PRODUCT GUIDE

■ **EUCALYPTUS:**

Properties:

— Expectorant.
— Anti-catarrhal.
— Parasite removing.

Applications:

— Pharyngitis, bronchitis, asthma, sinusitis, and flu.
— Diabetes.
— Parasitic infections.

Dosage:

— 1 capsule with each meal.

■ **FENNEL:**

— Fennel's main virtue is that it is an excellent remedy against gases.
— It essentially relieves intestinal pain from digestion and flatulence, and also encourages appetite.
— Fennel is useful in the treatment of several gastric ailments in which a stimulating effect is sought.
— It is a mild expectorant and is indicated in the treatment of chronic coughs.
— The root has diuretic properties.
— The leaf promotes wound healing and stimulates gastric motility.
— Anti-bacterial effect.
— Useful in glaucoma because it reduces intraocular pressure.
— Reduces blood cholesterol levels.
— Used to fight anemia due to its high iron content.
— Favors menstruation and relieves the menstrual pain.

Properties:

— Helps to eliminate intestinal gases.
— Antiseptic.
— Mucolytic (dissolves mucus).
— Expectorant.
— Diuretic.
— Helps fight bad breath.
— Anti-rheumatic.

201

— Antioxidant.

Contraindications:

— Contraindicated in those with estrogen deficiency.

Dosage:

— 3-6 capsules with each meal.

## ■ FENUTHYME (THYME AND FENUGREEK):

Properties:

— Respiratory decongestant.
— Reduces the absorption of sugars and fats.

Indications:

— Respiratory ailments.
— Weight-loss diets.

Dosage:

— 2 capsules, 2-3 times daily with meals.

## ■ FOLIC ACID (VITAMIN B9)

Properties:

— Stimulates appetite and the formation of hydrochloric acid.
— Helps proper liver function.
— Emotional stabilizer.
— Delays the onset of gray hair (together with vitamin B5).
— Prevents fetal problems.
— Helps to detoxify malonic acid from the kidneys.

Indications:

— Weakness and fatigue.
— Irritability and insomnia.
— Poor memory.
— Reduced kidney function.
— Anemia.

Dosage:

— 1 capsule with 1 or 2 meals.

# CLARK THERAPY PRODUCT GUIDE

■ **GARLIC ODORLESS (extract):**

Properties:

— Antibiotic, useful in the prevention and treatment of infectious diseases.
— Prevents intestinal fermentation processes.
— Vasodilator and relaxant.
— Prevents premature aging.
— Improves the oxygenation of tissues.
— Promotes reduction of the amount of glucose in blood.
— Decreases arterial hypertension.
— Prevents the emergence of intestinal parasites.
— Helps to expel heavy metals and other toxins from the body.

Dosage:

— 1 capsule with each meal.

■ **GINGER (root):**

Properties:

— Antiseptic
— Fever reducer
— Cough suppressant.
— Carminative (stimulates gastric motility)
— Anti-ulcer
— Anti-emetic (stops or prevents vomiting).
— Respiratory and cardiac analeptic (stimulant).
— Anti-convulsant
— Hypotensive
— Cardiac sedative.
— Kidney detoxicant.

Indications:

— Flu, pharyngitis, rhinitis, and angina.
— Low appetite and slow digestion.
— Dizziness, light-headedness, diarrhea, and rheumatic pains.
— Bloating (gases).
— Difficult digestion.
— In kidney cleanses, it helps to eliminate malonic acid from the kidneys.

203

Dosage:

— 1-3 capsules per day.

- **GINKGO BILOBA (extract):**

Properties:

— Antioxidant.
— Beneficial for problems with the brain, nervous system, and eyes.
— Helps memory.
— Helps premenstrual syndrome.

Indications:

— Circulatory and capillary permeability problems.
— Alzheimer's and disorders of the brain and nervous system.
— Premenstrual syndrome and vascular erectile dysfunction.
— Concentration or memory problems, loss of physical performance, fatigue, headache, dizziness, depression, anxiety.

Dosage:

— 1-3 capsules per day on an empty stomach.

- **GINSENG (KOREAN) (extract):**

Properties:

— Promotes immunity against colds, flu, and other infections.
— Stimulates the immune system.
— Stimulates the mind.
— Improves the overall feeling of well-being.
— Improves sleep.
— Beneficial for stress and fatigue.
— Promotes mental activity and learning.
— Helps improve sexual potency.
— Beneficial for athletes in general.
— Beneficial for those with cholesterol problems and diabetes.
— Korean ginseng has greater effectiveness against fatigue.

# CLARK THERAPY PRODUCT GUIDE

Contraindications:

—      Please consult with a professional before taking this product if you are pregnant or nursing, taking any medication or planning a medical procedure.

Dosage:

— 1-3 capsules per day with meals.

## ■ GLUTAMIC ACID:

Properties:

— Increases the excitability of the neurons in the central nervous system.
— Acts both in the brain and in the spinal cord.
— GABA precursor.
— Anti-convulsant and painkiller.

Indications:

— Prostatic hyperplasia.
— Epilepsy and neuronal disorders.
— Motor disorders.

Dosage:

— 1-2 g, 20 minutes before each meal.

## ■ GLUTAMINE:

Indications:

— Intense physical training.
— Strengthens the immune system.
— Recovery from injuries.
— Prolonged stress.
— Tissue cell regeneration.
— Protein deficiency.
— Intestinal health.

Dosage:

— 2-10 capsules per day between meals, or 20 minutes before meals.

## ■ GLUTATHIONE:

205

# CLARK THERAPY PRODUCT GUIDE

Properties:

- Strengthens the immune system.
- Cellular detoxification (heavy metals, benzene).
- Liver protector.

Applications:

- Infections.
- Allergies.
- Degenerative and neoplastic diseases in general.
- Prevents cellular oxidation and anomalous changes of cells.
- Poisoning.

Dosage:

- 1-3 capsules per day. Can be dosed much higher therapeutically (up to 20 capsules).

- **GOLDENROD (tincture):**

Properties:

- Kidney detoxicant.

Indications:

- Use as directed in the Kidney Cleanse.

- **GREEN TEA (extract):**

Properties:

- Cardiorespiratory and nervous system stimulant.
- Diuretic.
- Venotonic and vasoprotective.
- Induces relaxation at the bronchial and urethral level and the bile ducts.
- Helps to burn body fat.
- Inhibits the growth of cancer cells.
- Antioxidant.
- Contains polyphenols that have been shown to be effective in a number of diseases

Indications:

- Physical and mental fatigue.

For more information on Dr. Hulda Clark visit www.drclark.net

# CLARK THERAPY PRODUCT GUIDE

— Diarrhea.
— Bronchitis.
— Asthma.
— Hemochromatosis (excess iron in the blood).
— Degenerative disorders.
— Weight loss.

Contraindications:

— Pregnant or lactating women should consult a health care provider before use.

Dosage:

— 1 capsule before 1 to 3 meals a day.

■ **HYDRANGEA (root) (capsules or powder):**

Properties:

— Diuretic.
— Laxative.
— Prevents the formation of stones.
— Supports kidney function.
— Stimulates the immune system due to its high content of organic germanium (an essential food for white blood cells).

Indications:

— Urinary infections.
— Prostate infections.
— Kidney stones.

Dosage:

— 1-2 capsules (or 500-1000 mg powder), 3-5 times per day with meals.

■ **HCL (hydrochloric acid):**

Indications:

— Insufficient stomach acid.
— Insufficient digestion of proteins.
— Infections of the digestive system.

<u>Dosage:</u>

— 5-10 drops at each meal (always in an empty capsule prepared at the moment of ingestion).

## ■ INOSITOL:

<u>Properties:</u>

— Reduces blood cholesterol.
— Essential for metabolizing fat.
— Stimulates hair growth.
— Liver protector.
— Painkiller

<u>Indications:</u>

— Depression.
— Panic attacks.
— Anxiety.
— Diabetes.
— Liver disorders.
— Arteriosclerosis.
— High cholesterol.
— Skin rashes.
— Degenerative disorders.

<u>Dosage:</u>

— 1 capsule, 2-3 times per day (depending on the case), preferably between meals.

## ■ IP6 (INOSITOL HEXAPHOSPHATE OR PHYTIC ACID):

<u>Properties:</u>

— Helps clean stones, calcifications, and metals from the colon, liver, brain, kidneys, heart, and gallbladder.
— Extracts radioactivity from the body.
— Cleans arteries.
— Immunostimulant.
— Helps to detoxify polonium and other heavy metals from the immune system and the entire body.

— Increases organ oxygenation (by transporting twice the as much oxygen as hemoglobin).

Indications:

— Degenerative disorders.
— Immune deficiencies.
— Increase of oxygenation in athletes and the sick.

Dosage:

— From 5 drops 3 times per day to 20 drops 5 times per day. At least 45 minutes before meals and other supplements.

■ **IRON (ferrous gluconate):**

Properties:

— Increases resistance to stress and illness.
— Provides strength and physical stamina.
— Promotes physical growth.
— Prevents anemia.
— Prevents infections of the respiratory system, as well as the teeth, ears, and skin.

Notice:

— Accidental overdose of iron-containing products is a leading cause of fatal poisoning in children under 6 years of age. Keep this product out of reach of children. In case of accidental overdose, call a doctor or poison control center immediately.

Dosage:

— 1 capsule per day with a main meal.

■ **KIDNEY HERBS:**

Properties:

— Strengthen the immune system.
— Cellular detoxification (heavy metals, benzene).
— Liver protector.
— Kidney detoxicant.

Indications:

— Infections.
— Allergies.
— Degenerative and neoplastic diseases in general.
— Prevents cellular oxidation and anomalous changes of cells.
— Poisoning.
— Kidney burdened with metabolic waste.

Applications:

— Part of the Kidney Cleanse.

## ■ LIPASE & PANCREATIN:

Properties:

— Helps in the digestion of carbohydrates and fats.

Applications:

— Digestive aid.

Dosage:

— 1-2 capsules with each meal.

## ■ LIVER HERBS

Properties:

— Simulant, detoxicant, and liver regenerator.

Dosage:

— 3 cups of tea per day.

## ■ LUGOL'S IODINE:

Properties:

— Antiseptic.

Applications:

— Bacterial infections, especially Salmonellas and Shigellas.

Contraindications:

— Do not use if allergic to iodine.

Dosage:

— 6 drops dissolved in water, 3-6 times per day before meals. Keep apart from other supplements, as Lugol's iodine will oxidize them.

## ■ LYSINE (capsules or powder):

Properties:

— Increases the synthesis of proteins.
— Improves the metabolism of carbohydrates and fatty acids.
— Promotes the absorption of calcium in the bone matrix.
— Possesses an anti-aging effect.
— Prevents the formation of kidney stones.
— Stimulates the production of antibodies.
— Stimulates growth hormone.
— Improves athletic performance.
— Prevents the absorption of arginine (essential for the Herpes virus).

Indications:

— Herpes simplex and genital Herpes.
— Hair loss.
— Anemia.

Dosage:

— 2-10 capsules (or 1-5 g powder) per day, between meals.

## ■ MAGNESIUM OXIDE:

Properties:

— Regulates blood cholesterol.
— Regulates blood sugar level.
— Helps vitamin and mineral assimilation.
— Functions as an intracellular mineral that is essential for the transmission of nerve impulses.
— Works to repair and maintain organ cells and tissues.
— Helps with organ growth.
— Fundamental in the processes of muscular contraction and relaxation.
— Promotes the correct utilization of vitamins B, C, and E.
— Facilitates the dissolving of kidney stones.

Dosage:

— 2 capsules before a meal.

## ■ MANGANESE:

Properties:

— Promotes the synthesis of fatty acids and cholesterol.
— Promotes optimal development of the skeleton and the fetus.
— Essential in the formation of cartilage.
— Helps in the synthesis of thyroid hormones.
— Promotes the elimination of ammonia.
— Promotes fertility.

Indications:

— Dizziness.
— Seizures.
— Hearing loss.
— Tinnitus.
— Blindness.
— Heart problems.
— Diabetes.
— Bone problems.
— Rheumatoid arthritis.

Dosage:

— 1 capsule daily with a meal.

## ■ METHIONINE:

Properties:

— Helps the liver to process fats.
— Reduces histamine in blood (anti-allergic effect).

Indications:

— Allergies.
— Pancreatitis.
— Liver support.
— Schizophrenia.
— Supports kidney function.

For more information on Dr. Hulda Clark visit www.drclark.net

— Helps to detoxify malonic acid from the kidneys.

Dosage:

— 2-4 capsules per day (depending on body weight), preferably 20 minutes before meals.

## ▪ MINT OIL:

Properties:

— Reduces stomach acidity and soothes the stomach.
— Inhaling it on a cloth or tissue relieves colds, flu, cough, bronchitis, sinusitis, headaches, and toothaches.

Indications:

— Indigestion, gas, headaches, menstrual irregularity, sinusitis.
— Infectious illnesses of the liver and gallbladder.

Dosage for internal use:

— 2-3 drops, 2 to 3 times per day.

## ▪ MSM:

Properties:

— Regenerator of connective tissue.
— Anti-inflammatory and analgesic (pain relief).
— Immunostimulant.
— Skin detoxicant.
— General antioxidant, as well as brain antioxidant.
— Breaks the chain of the process of cancerous formations.
— Converts ferric iron (harmful) to ferrous iron (beneficial) within the human body.
— Helps in the removal of asbestos from the body.
— Increases cellular permeability: this leads to greater removal of toxins and greater absorption of vitamins and minerals.
— Deactivates toxins and enables their elimination.
— One of the few antioxidants that crosses the blood-brain barrier (protecting against excessive oxidation in the brain).

Indications:

— Arthritis and rheumatism.

— Arthrosis.
— Allergies.
— Acne.
— Promotes concentration.
— Increases oxygen absorption.
— Regulates autoimmune processes.
— Detoxification of metals.
— Cancer and other degenerative diseases.
— Iron deficiency anemia.
— Reduces anxiety and depression.
— Acts against fungi, bacteria, and parasites.
— Especially good for children.
— Marked effectiveness in muscle pains and cramps.
— Similar effectiveness to aspirin or codeine as an analgesic.
— Regarding gastritis with hyperacidity, the use of antacids and H2 blockers can be reduced or even stopped.
— Beneficial for the skin and hair (acne, eczema, dryness, etc.).

Dosage:

— 2-6 capsules per day, 20 minutes before meals.

## ■ MULTIVITAMIN

Properties:

— Helps to maintain the immune system.
— Helps to maintain healthy hair and skin.
— Prevents mild vitamin deficiencies.

Indications:

— For general prevention and covering the body's basic needs.
— Decline in performance of the immune system.
— Stress.
— Skin and/or hair problems.

Dosage:

— 2 capsules per day.

# CLARK THERAPY PRODUCT GUIDE

■ **NUTMEG OIL:**

Properties:

— Digestive, appetite stimulant.
— Antiseptic.
— Nervous system stimulant.

Indications:

— Slow digestion.
— Halitosis (bad breath).
— Gallstones.
— Dysmenorrhea (menstrual pain).
— Rheumatism.
— Diarrhea.

Dosage:

— 2-3 drops, 2-3 times per day.

■ **SUPER OMEGA 3 (essential fatty acids):**

Properties:

— Help to regulate the coagulation index in the blood.
— Nourish skin and hair cells.
— Protect the myelin in nerve cells.
— Help to prevent deposits of cholesterol in the arteries and reduce the level of triglycerides.
— Facilitate the transport of oxygen to cells, tissues, and organs.
— Promote the elimination of saturated fats from the body.
— Regulate the adrenal and thyroid glands.
— Keep the mucus and nerve membranes healthy.
— Help to maintain calcium, phosphorus, and vitamin A levels.

Dosage:

— 1-3 softgels per day with meals.

■ **OREGANO OIL:**

Properties:

— Antiseptic.
— Anti-fungal (including yeast).

For more information on Dr. Hulda Clark visit www.drclark.net

— Analgesic.
— Anti-viral.
— Parasite purging.
— Anti-bacterial (including E. coli, Streptococci, Staphylococci, etc.)
— Anti-inflammatory.
— Antioxidant.

Indications:

— Candidiasis and other fungal infections: internal use.
— Athlete's foot: topical use, lightly diluted in water.
— Painkiller for mild degenerative disorders.
— Gastrointestinal problems resulting from bacterial or fungal build-up (indigestion, gas, bloating, pain in the digestive tract).
— Pharyngitis, otitis, sinusitis.
— Asthma.
— Dysmenorrhea and amenorrhea.
— For external use, it is beneficial in varicose veins, joint problems, and skin infections (slightly diluted in water).
— Pains of all sorts.

Dosage:

— Pour it in an empty capsule and always consume with food.
— 3-5 drops, 2-3 times per day with meals.

### ■ ORNITHINE:

Properties:

— Helps to eliminate ammonia from the body.
— Helps to metabolize excess body fat.
— Facilitates sleep and relaxation.

Dosage:

— 2-8 capsules before going to bed.

### ■ PAPAIN:

Properties:

— Natural anti-inflammatory.
— Parasite remover (against Ascaris and pinworms).

For more information on Dr. Hulda Clark visit www.drclark.net

Dosage:

— 5 capsules on an empty stomach, 3 times per day (for parasite removal and anti-inflammatory effects).

## ■ PAU D'ARCO (Tabebuia):

Properties:

— Immunostimulant.
— Anti-fungal.
— Antibiotic.
— Analgesic.
— Anti-bacterial.

Indications:

— Candidiasis.
— Bacterial infections.
— Rheumatic ailments.
— Psoriasis.

Dosage:

— 2 capsules with each meal.

## ■ PEPSIN:

Properties:

— Required for the optimal digestion of proteins.
— Helps to eliminate prions in degenerative patients.

Dosage:

— 2 capsules with each meal.

## ■ POTASSIUM (CITRATE):

Properties:

— Helps to regulate organ hydration.
— Stimulates nerve impulses.
— Helps with cerebral oxygenation.

Indications:

— Hypertension.

217

— Edemas.
— Muscular weakness.
— Nerve paralysis.

Notice:

— Consumed excessively, can lead to heart arrhythmia. If you suffer from heart arrhythmia, consult with a doctor before taking potassium supplements.

Dosage:

— 4 capsules daily with a main meal.

■ **QUASSIA:**

Properties:

— Digestive system tonic.
— Digestive painkiller.
— Parasite removing, anti-bacterial, anti-fungal, and anti-viral.

Indications:

— Stomach pain.
— Ulcers.
— Lack of appetite.
— Constipation.
— Liver congestion.
— Infections.
— Anti-malarial.

Notice:

— Not to be used during pregnancy.

Dosage:

— 1-2 g, 2-3 times per day before meals.

■ **QUERCETIN (WITH BROMELAIN):**

Properties:

— Natural anti-histamine.
— Anti-inflammatory.
— Protects the stomach from ulcers and gastric distress.

— Inhibitor of cancer cells and oral tumors.
— Stops excessive cell growth in bone marrow (leukemia).
— Bioflavonoid. Strengthens capillary walls.

Indications:

— Useful for seasonal and food allergies.
— Asthma.
— Allergic rhinitis.
— Antioxidant.
— Inflammatory processes.
— Degenerative disorders.

Dosage:

— 1 capsule with each meal.

## ◼ REISHI MUSHROOM:

Properties:

— Helps to boost the immune system.
— Promotes the proper functioning of the circulatory system and nervous system.
— Anti-bacterial agent.
— Anti-inflammatory.
— Antioxidant.
— Anti-allergic.
— Blood sugar regulator.
— Stress reducer.

Dosage:

— 2-6 capsules per day with meals.

## ◼ ROSE HIPS (ROSA CANINA):

Properties:

— Due to its abundance of organic vitamin C, it increases the body's resistance to infections.
— Immunostimulant.
— Anti-diarrheal.
— Scars wounds.
— Diuretic.

— Helps to detoxify malonic acid from the kidneys.

Indications:

- Diarrhea.
- Capillary fragility.
- Edemas.
- Varicose veins and hemorrhoids.
- Infections and degenerative diseases.
- Supports kidney function.

Dosage:

- 1 capsule with breakfast, lunch, and dinner; this dosage can be increased as much as desired.

## ■ SAW PALMETTO (extract):

Properties:

- Anti-edematous.
- Problems in the prostate and the production of testosterone.
- Asthma and bronchitis.

Dosage:

- 2-3 capsules per day, with meals.

## ■ SELENIUM:

Properties:

- Contributes to proper liver functioning.
- Boosts the immune system, feeding the white blood cells.
- Protects the body from the effects of toxic elements.
- Helps with male reproductive functions.
- Anti-inflammatory.
- Protects against free radicals.
- Protects against degenerative disorders, arthritis, and coronary diseases.
- Antioxidant.
- Maintains the elasticity of the body tissues.
- Increases the production of antibodies.

Dosage:

— 1 capsule daily with a meal.

### ■ SLIPPERY ELM (in powder)

Properties:

— Anti-diarrheal.
— Anti-inflammatory.
— Intestinal pain reliever.
— Relieves joint pain.

Indications:

— Undernourishment.
— Intestinal and digestive problems.
— Gastroenteritis.
— Constipation in children.
— Crohn's Disease and irritable bowel syndrome.
— External application against skin fungi.

Dosage:

— 1-3 teaspoons or capsules, 1-3 times per day.

### ■ SODIUM ALGINATE:

Properties:

— Chelator: eliminates heavy metals from the blood, mainly strontium.
— Helps inflammatory intestinal problems. Dosage:
— 1-2 teaspoons per day.

### ■ SODIUM BICARBONATE:

Indications:

— Metabolic acidosis.
— Alkalizer.

Dosage:

— ¼ tablespoon dissolved in a glass of water, both when you wake up and at bedtime.

■ **ST. JOHN'S WORT (Hypericum perforatum):**

Properties:

— Antidepressant.
— Nervous system stabilizer.

Notice:

Persons with a medical condition or taking monoamine oxidase (MAO) inhibitors should consult a health professional before taking this product. Hypericin causes the skin and eyes to become photosensitive. Avoid lengthy exposure to strong sunlight and other sources of ultraviolet light while taking this product. Consult with your health professional before using St. John's Wort if you are taking any prescription medications.

Dosage:

— 1 capsule with each meal.

■ **TAURINE (capsules or powder):**

Properties:

— Promotes the proper functioning of the heart, muscles, and nervous system.
— Promotes brain development.
— Helps with the formation of bile.
— Promotes the production of white blood cells.
— Prevents dementia, senility, and Alzheimer's.
— Increases the body's resistance to infections.
— Promotes sleep.
— Prevents fatty liver disease.
— Helps regulate blood sugar levels.

Dosage:

— 1-3 capsules (or 500-1500 mg powder) 20 minutes before 2 meals.

■ **THIOCTIC ACID OR ALPHA-LIPOIC-ACID:**

Properties:

— Antioxidant.
— Protector and regenerator of nervous tissue.
— Producer of cellular energy.

— Eliminator of heavy metals and other toxins.
— Reducer of transaminases and liver regenerator.
— Immunostimulant (since it is an interferon propellant).

Indications:

— As an antioxidant, detoxicant, and liver regenerator.
— Also used in: hepatitis, cancer, multiple sclerosis, amyotrophic lateral sclerosis (ALS), Alzheimer's, AIDS, and diabetes.

Dosage:

— 1 capsule with each meal.

## ■ TURMERIC:

Properties:

— The therapeutic uses of turmeric include fighting liver diseases, especially those that result in jaundice, cholecystitis (inflammation of the gallbladder), biliary colic, and dyspepsia. One's appetite often returns, which is commonly lacking in these types of diseases. It should not be used if you also suffer from stomach ulcers or intestinal bleeding.

Indications:

— Hepatobiliary problems, hepatitis.
— Liver protector.
— Prevents thromboembolism. Improves circulation.
— Cholelithiasis (gallstones).
— Cholecystitis (inflammation of the gallbladder).
— Bacterial infections.
— Inflammations of all sorts.

Dosage:

— 2-3 capsules with each meal.

## ■ TRYPTOPHAN:

Properties:

— Regulates the level of serotonin in the brain, promoting relaxation.
— Helps with the formation of proteins.
— Reduces appetite.
— Controls mood, maintains a good mood.

223

— Helps tolerating of pain from physical activity.
— Necessary for fetal growth.
— Necessary for nitrogen balance in adults.

## Dosage:

— 1-3 capsules, 20 minutes before dinner.

## ■ UVA URSI:

## Properties:

— Anti-bacterial of the urinary system and kidney protector.
— Anti-inflammatory.
— Anti-viral.
— Antioxidant.
— Detoxicant of malonic acid in kidneys (which is the principal cause of kidney failure).

## Dosage:

— 1-3 capsules before each meal.

## ■ VALERIAN (root extract):

## Properties:

— Balances the nervous system (sedative, anti-convulsant, and mild hypotensive).

## Indications:

— Anxiety, insomnia, depression, and abnormally rapid heart rate.
— Headaches, hypertension, irritable bowel.
— Gastrointestinal spasms, gastric pains.

## Notice:

May cause drowsiness. Do not use when driving a motor vehicle or operating machinery. Do not use if you are taking sedatives or tranquilizers without first consulting a health professional.

## Dosage:

— 1 capsule 3-6 times throughout the day or near bedtime.

# CLARK THERAPY PRODUCT GUIDE

■ **VITAMIN A:**

Properties:

— Protects against infections.
— Essential for good eye health.
— Protects the skin, maintaining its elasticity.
— Improves the synthesis of proteins.
— Maintains healthy bones.
— Prevents anemia and promotes growth.
— Removes age spots.
— Promotes the development of strong bones, skin, hair, teeth, and gums.
— Participates in the synthesis of RNA.

Dosage:

— 1-2 capsules per day with a main meal.

■ **VITAMIN B COMPLEX:**

Properties:

— Facilitates the conversion of carbohydrates into glucose.
— Vital for the metabolism of fats and proteins.
— Essential for the proper functioning of the nervous system.
— Essential for the maintenance of muscle tone and the intestinal tract.
— Essential for the health of skin, hair, eyes, mouth, and liver.

Dosage:

— 1 capsule daily at breakfast or lunch.

■ **VITAMIN B1 (thiamine):**

Properties:

— Helps with the metabolism of carbohydrates.
— Beneficial effect on nerves.
— Improves mental state and increases learning capacity.
— Improves the muscular development of the stomach, intestine, and heart.
— Essential for stabilizing appetite, improving digestion and assimilating food.
— Helps to prevent arteriosclerosis.

225

Dosage:

— 1 capsule per day with a main meal.

■ **VITAMIN B2 (riboflavin) (capsules or powder):**

Properties:

— Helps with the assimilation of carbohydrates, fats, and proteins.
— Necessary for cellular respiration and for healthy skin, hair, and nails.
— Helps with growth and reproduction.
— Promotes good eye health.
— Helps to regulate organ acidity.
— Helps to eliminate benzene from the body, increasing the effectiveness of the immune system.
— Improves circulation.
— Helps in the production of red blood cells.
— Helps in the detoxification of malonic acid in the kidneys.
— Helps in the detoxification of chlorine, isopropyl alcohol, PCBs, toluene, and xylene.

Dosage:

— 1 capsule per day (or 300 mg powder) with one of the main meals.

■ **VITAMIN B3 (niacin):**

Properties:

— Improves circulation.
— Controls cholesterol.
— Regulates the nervous system.
— Useful for dermatitis.

Dosage:

— 1-2 capsules per day.

■ **VITAMIN B3 (niacinamide):**

— Active form of vitamin B3.
— Greater absorption than niacin.

Dosage:

— 1-2 capsules per day with meals.

- **VITAMIN B5 (pantothenic acid):**

Properties:

- — Improves adrenal function.
- — Increases tolerance to stress.
- — Helps to prevent premature aging.
- — Supports the immune system.
- — Prevents arthritis.
- — Helps to detoxify malonic acid from the kidneys.

Indications:

- — Allergies.
- — Exhaustion.
- — Stress.
- — Weakened immune system.
- — Nervous system abnormalities.
- — Bruxism (excessive grinding of teeth and/or clenching of the jaw).
- — Supports kidney function.

Dosage:

- — 1 capsule with one of the main meals.

- **VITAMIN B6 (pyridoxine):**

Properties:

- — Helps with enzymatic synthesis.
- — Plays a role in the synthesis of hemoglobin.
- — Helps to metabolize fat.
- — Aids in the production of hydrochloric acid.
- — Transports amino acids inside of cells.
- — Regulates and facilitates the ability to fall asleep.
- — Helps maintain the balance between sodium and potassium.
- — Facilitates the release of glycogen in the liver and muscles for energy production in the body.
- — Helps to dissolve kidney stones.
- — Helps in the detoxification of malonic acid in the kidneys.
- — Helps to eliminate aluminum.

Dosage:

- — 1 capsule per day with a main meal.

- **VITAMIN B7 (biotin):**

Properties:

— Essential in the metabolism of carbohydrates, proteins, and fats.
— Helps to keep hair and skin healthy.
— Essential for nerve health. Indications:
— Fatigue and depression.
— Skin problems, eczema, dermatitis, etc.
— High cholesterol.

Dosage:

— 1 capsule with one of the main meals.

- **VITAMIN B12 (cobalamine):**

Properties:

— Essential for normal metabolism of nerve tissue.
— Helps in the metabolism of carbohydrates, proteins, and fats.
— Works with other vitamins, minerals, and amino acids for proper organ functioning.
— Necessary for DNA synthesis.
— Helps in the metabolism of fatty acids.
— Cell detoxicant.
— Participates in the formation of blood.
— Promotes growth and increases appetite.
— Keeps the nervous system healthy.
— Helps in the detoxification of malonic acid in the kidneys.

Dosage:

— 1 capsule with one of the main meals.

- **VITAMIN C (ascorbic acid) (capsules and powder):**

Properties:

— Promotes formation of collagen and connective tissue.
— Helps to heal wounds and burns.
— Promotes the formation of red blood cells, preventing bleeding.
— Fights viral and bacterial infections.
— Reduces the incidence of blood clots.
— Helps in the metabolism of amino acids.
— Protects against carcinogens.
— Helps in the metabolism of calcium.

— Antioxidant.
— Promotes iron absorption.
— Regulates cholesterol levels in the blood.
— Helps in the formation of teeth and bones.
— Keeps the blood capillaries and sexual organs healthy.
— Anti-histamine (prevention of allergic reactions).
— Organ detoxicant of harmful substances.
— Strengthens the immune system.
— Promotes longevity.
— Helps detoxify malonic acid in the kidneys.

Dosage:

— Up to 1-2 capsules (or 1-2 g powder) with each meal.

■ **VITAMIN C (BUFFERED) (calcium ascorbate):**

— See vitamin C –acidity buffered by calcium.
— Suitable for people with gastric ulcers and gastritis.

Dosage:

— Up to 1-4 capsules with each meal.

■ **VITAMIN D (cholecalciferol):**

Properties:

— Helps with the absorption of calcium and phosphorus into the bones.
— Stabilizes the nervous and cardiac systems.
— Promotes proper blood clotting.
— Helps in enzymatic synthesis.

Dosage:

— 1-3 softgels per day with one of the main meals.

■ **VITAMIN E (tocopherol)**

Properties:

— Antioxidant.
— Improves the functioning of the male and female reproductive systems.
— Helps to assimilate vitamins.
— Helps in muscle oxygenation, increasing their strength and energy.
— Vasodilator.
— Prevents the formation of blood clots.

— Helps in cellular transport, strengthening the capillary membranes and protecting red blood cells.

Dosage:

— 1-3 softgels per day with meals.

## ■ WORMWOOD:

Properties:

— Anthelmintic.
— Antibiotic.
— Emmenagogue.
— Expectorant.
— Carminative.
— Easily penetrates the brain and bone marrow to combat parasites in these organs.
— Attacks parasite larvae.
— Highly toxic for cancer cells, but not for healthy cells (it is selective).
— The Chinese used it to fight the malaria parasite.
— Attacks the intermediate phases of Fasciolopsis buski, which produce tumor growth factor.
— When in contact with cellular iron, it produces a chemical reaction that releases free radicals that break the cell membranes. Remember that the parasite has high quantities of iron. Also, cancer needs a large amount of iron to replicate its DNA when it divides, and this is the reason that wormwood works as an anti-tumor agent (a breast cancer cell contains around 15 times more transferrin than a healthy cell).
— Very good results in leukemia, especially due to the extremely high level of iron contained in cells infected with this disease.

Indications:

— In parasite removal programs.

Dosage:

— Up to 9 capsules per day.

## ■ ZINC (gluconate):

Properties:

— Necessary for the production of hormones and insulin.
— Immune system stimulant.
— Liver protector.

# CLARK THERAPY PRODUCT GUIDE

Indications:

— Stress.
— White stains on the nails.
— Sterility and impotence.
— Impaired glucose tolerance.

Dosage:

— 1 capsule with one of the main meals.

For more information on Dr. Hulda Clark visit www.drclark.net

# DIRECTORY OF CLARK THERAPISTS

## UNITED STATES

### Natural Biological Medicine
Dr. Michael Clarjen-Arconada
P.O. Box 828
Sag Harbor, NY 11963 – USA
P +1-305-926 9679
CLARK THERAPIST

### Natural Herbal Therapy
Lucinda Robinson
815 A Wynnshire Drive
Hickory, NC 28601 – USA
P +1-828-385 0609
CLARK THERAPIST

### Jenks Health Team
Dr. Gerald Wootan
715 West Main Street
Jenks, OK 74037 – USA
P +1-918-299-9447
F +1-918-299-5325
CLARK THERAPIST

### Judy Kemecsei
Sherman Oaks, CA 91403 – USA
P +1-818-789-1698
CLARK THERAPIST

## CANADA

### Christine Nelson, ND
.P.344
St-Adolphe-d'Howard
Quebec J0T 2B0 – Canada
P +1-819-327 2422
CLARK THERAPIST

# DIRECTORY OF CLARK THERAPISTS

**Angelica and Gloria Ertel**
Health In-Sync
42 Royal Park Blvd.
Barrie, ON L4N 6M8 – Canada
P +1-705-503 6125
SYNCROMETER TESTER AND CLARK THERAPIST

## LATIN AMERICA

**Mauricio Rivera**
4451 La Paz – Bolivia
P +591-70-111 540
CLARK THERAPIST

**Ing. Jorge Nunez Sotillo**
Ter. Sonia Carbajal Torres
Calle Cantuarias 140 Of 228
Miraflores, Lima 18 – Peru
P +51-1-241 8325
CLARK THERAPIST

**Instituto Internacional de Odontología Holística, Medicina Biológica y Sanación Genética Cósmica – Dr. Rubén Dario Diaz Granados García**
Mna 5, Lote 1, 3a Etapa, 2° piso, esquina
Las Gaviotas, Cartagena de Indias – Colombia
P +57-300-210 8593; +57-310-364 9614; +57-317-742 9742
DIAGNÓSTICO Y TRATAMIENTO BIOLÓGICO DE TODO TIPO DE CÁNCER Y DE OTRAS ENFERMEDADES SEGÚN LA DRA. CLARK

## AUSTRALIA AND ASIA

**Vincent Coyte**
Hobart, TAS – Australia
P +61-(0)40-850 6230
SYNCROMETER TESTER AND THERAPIST

233

# DIRECTORY OF CLARK THERAPISTS

**Dr. William H. van Ewijk, M.D.,M.A.**
The Placenta Research Foundation – Biologics International
10 Anson Road #15-14 International Plaza
Singapore 079903 – Singapore
P +31-320-247 326
F +31-320-247-327
CLARK THERAPIST

**Better Health Research Centre – Richard Wachter**
Box 133
Rarotonga – Cook Islands
P +682-24 940
SYNCROMETER TESTER

## AFRICA

**Shelley Keith**
PO Box 20006
3290 Horwic– South Africa
P +27-033-330 7613
F +27-086-7433910
CLARK THERAPIST

**Ben Ashoori**
ICM Industries
7-73 Capital Hill Estate
1585 Midrand– South Africa
P +27 11 312 3393
F +27 11 312 4877
CLARK THERAPIST

## EUROPE

**Battersea Back Clinic – Hillary Kennedy**
4 Ransomes Dock, 35-37 Parkgate Road
LONDON SW11 4NP – United Kingdom
P +44(0)207-350 0938; +44(0)797-900 2310
CLARK THERAPIST

# DIRECTORY OF CLARK THERAPISTS

**Sollucidus – Margit Kuiper**
Klinkenberg 26
6231BD Meerssen, Limburg– The Netherlands
P +31-(0)62-547 5941
F +31-143-321 9668
SYNCROMETER TESTER AND CLARK THERAPIST

**Heike Beckers-Glatzel**
Schoren 27
3635 Oberhofen am Thunersee – Switzerland
www.sanavital.ch
P +41-31-312 2126
F +41-31-312 2127
SYNCROMETER TESTER AND CLARK THERAPIST

**Dr. Ph.D. Silvia Albicocchi**
Studio Alternativne Medicine Metoda Clark D.O.O.
Partizanska cesta 33b
6210 Sezana – Slovenia (Italy)
P +39-333-893 2888
Visits regularly in Milano, Rome and San Marino
SYNCROMETER TESTER AND CLARK THERAPIST

**Dr. Peter Schreiber**
Medico Chirurgo - Specialista in Dermatologia e Venereologia
Piazza Diaz, 2
60123 Ancona – Italy
P +39-335-525 2513
F +39-071-201 788
BIOENERGETIC TESTER AND CLARK THERAPIST

**Patricia Joud**
1, rue Bossuet
69006 Lyon – France
Tel.: ++33-4-78 65 06 24
patricia.joud@gmail.com

# DIRECTORY OF CLARK THERAPISTS

---

**GERMANY**

**Dr. Med Horst Tippenhauer**
Luitpoldstrasse 1A
63897 Miltenberg – Germany
P +49-9371-906 22
F +49-9371-906 23
BIOENERGETIC TESTER AND CLARK THERAPIST

---

**Alan Baklayan, HP**
Unterer Anger 16
80331 München – Germany
P +49-89-260 92 27
F +49-89-260 261 72
BIOENERGETIC TESTER AND CLARK THERAPIST

---

**Corinna Shimmels, HP**
Danziger Strasse 5
23564 Lübeck – Germany
P +49-451-400 7089
F +49-451-400 7090
SYNCROMETER TESTER AND CLARK THERAPIST

---

**Naturheilpraxis Sonnenbaum**
Heilpraktiker Peter Schmidt
Von-Stauffenberg-Strasse 21
82008 Unterhaching – Germany
P +49-89-6146 5445
F +49-89-6655 0716
BIOENERGETIC TESTER AND CLARK THERAPIST

---

**Naturheilpraxis Dipl.-W.J.Karl-Heinz Hanusch**
Ingwerweg 8a
65191 Wiesbaden – Germany
P +49-611-561 323
F +49-611-957 0808
CLARK THERAPIST

# DIRECTORY OF CLARK THERAPISTS

**Andrea Lapp Schreiber**
Sanisoma Ganzheitsmedizin
Christian-Kremp-Str. 10a
35578 Wetzlar – Germany
P +49-2776-911 793
F +49-2776-913 0857
BIOENERGETIC TESTER AND CLARK THERAPIST

**Ernst Wössner, HP**
Allee 40
74072 Heilbronn– Germany
P +49-7131-598 150
CLARK THERAPIST

**Gabriele Brügmann**
Beschkamp 6
22964 Steinburg – Germany
P +49-4534-85 21
BIOENERGETIC TESTER AND CLARK THERAPIST

**Uschi Ausfelder, HP**
Albert-Schweitzer-Strasse 10
84539 Ampfing – Germany
P +49-8636-695 832
SYNCROMETER TESTER AND CLARKTHERAPIST

**Praxis Zentrum Gabriela Frädrich, HP**
Bahnhofstrasse 48
85375 Neufahrn – Germany
P +49-8165-799 810
CLARK THERAPIST

237

# DIRECTORY OF CLARK THERAPISTS

**SPAIN**

**Ignacio Chamorro Balda**
Clark Institute
c/ Maudes, 15 – entreplanta A
28003 Madrid – Spain
Tel.: +34-91-441 1243
info@institutoclark.com
www.institutoclark.com

**Emilio Jesús Espejo**
c/ Virgen de Gracia, 11 – Bajo
Alhaurín El Grande, Málaga –Spain
Tel.: +34-952-596 511 / +34-607-672 725
fikios@yahoo.es

**María Teresa Conejo**
Avda. Inmaculada Concepción, 8
Arroyo de la miel, Málaga –Spain
Tel: +34-952-560 534
madretierramt@telefonica.net

**María Isabel González Domínguez**
c/ Concejal García Feo, 13
35011 Las Palmas de Gran Canaria – Spain
Tel: +34-928-250 844
maribel.nathan@yahoo.es

# HOLISTIC DENTISTS

**Frank Jerome, DDS**
Author of "The Tooth Truth", a book recommended by Dr. Hulda Clark
639 Washington Street
Columbus, IN 47201 – USA
P +1-812-376 8525

**John W. Johnson, DDS**
New Albany Adult Dentistry
5121 Forest Drive Suite A
New Albany, OH 43054 – USA
P +1-614-775 9300
naadultdentistry@gmail.com
www.columbusohiodentist.com

**Whole-Body Dentistry – Mark and Adam Breiner, DDS**
5520 Park Avenue, Suite 301
Fairfield, CT 06611 – USA
P +1-203-371 0300
F +1-203-365 8479
info@wholebodymed.com
www.wholebodymed.com

**Mitchell L. Marder, DDS**
9730 3rd Ave. NE, Ste. 205
Seattle, WA 98115 – USA
P +1-206 367 6453
F +1-206 367 4971
www.drmitchmarder.com

**Ray Behm Jr, DDS**
127 N Garden Ave
Clearwater, FL 33755 – USA
P +1-727-446 6747
AskDrBehm@SaveYourTeeth.com
www.saveyourteeth.com

# HOLISTIC DENTISTS

**Richard T. Hansen, DDS**
1031 Rosecrans Ave #104
Fullerton, CA 92833 – USA
P +1-714-870 0310
DrHansen@LaserDentalCenters.com
www.laserdentalcenters.com

**John Moreno, DDS**
6 Huges, Suite 100
Irvine, CA 92618 – USA
P +1-949-487 9220
www.ejohnmoreno.com

**Ezekiel N. Lagos, DDS**
P.O. Box 210513
Chula Vista, CA 91921 – USA
P +1-877-356 0056
F +52-6646-802 386
drlagos@biologicaldent.com
www.biologicaldent.com

**Oscar Solorio, DDS**
Avenida 5 de Mayo 964, Zona Centro
Tijuana, BC 22000 – Mexico
P +1-619-308 7830; +52-6646-853 973
F +52-6646-853 993
DrSolorio@gmail.com
www.drsolorio.com

**Benjamin Arechiga, DDS**
1310 Josefa Ortiz de Dominguez
Plaza Santa Fe, 2nd floor
Zona del Rio, Tijuana BC 22320 – Mexico
P +52-6646-829 464
info@bajadentistry.com
www.bajadentistry.com

# HOLISTIC DENTISTS

**Instituto Internacional de Odontología Holística, Medicina Biológica y Sanación Genética Cósmica – Dr. Rubén Dario Diaz Granados García**
Mna 5, Lote 1, 3a Etapa, 2° piso, esquina
Las Gaviotas
Cartagena de Indias – Colombia
P +57-300-210 8593; +57-310-364 9614; +57-317-742 9742

**ICM Industries – Ben Ashoori**
7-73 Capital Hill Estate
1585 Midrand – South Africa
P +27 11 312 3393
F +27 11 312 4877

**Dr. John Anderson, BDS – Gardenside Dental Center**
23 Victoria Gardens
SA11 3AY Neath Port Talbot, Wales – United Kingdom
P +44-1639-644 460
www.gdcneath.com

**Dr. John Roberts**
Cote Royd House
HD3 3AN Huddersfield – United Kingdom
P +44-1484-514 451
F +44-1706-712 935
info@crdentalpractice.co.uk
www.coteroyddentalpractice.co.uk

**Dr. med. dent. Herbert Dietrich**
via Tesserete 1
6900 Lugano – Switzerland
P +41-91-966 3636

**Dr. Dirk Eckhardt**
Haldenstrasse 1
6342 Baar – Switzerland
P +41-41-768 2466
ambi@paramed.ch
www.paramed.ch

241

# HOLISTIC DENTISTS

**Dr. med dent. Samuel Gerber – Zahnarztpraxis Belp**
Belpbergstrasse 1
3123 Belp – Switzerland
P +41-31-819 2096
info@zahnarztpraxis-belp.ch
www.zahnarztpraxis-belp.ch

**Dr. Ottaviano Tapparo**
Holistic Immunological Dentistry Specialist
Rosenkavalierplatz 18/IV
81925 München – Germany
P +49-89-9400 3415
info@natrail.de
www.natrail.de

**Dr. Julian Brandes**
Norbisrather Strasse 3
50739 Köln – Germany
P +49-221-599 1901
F +49-221-599 2675
info@vollkeramik-spezialist.de
www.vollkeramik-spezialist.de

**Dott. Francesco Guadagno**
via San Nicolò, 19
34121 Trieste – Italy
P +39-040-660 040
studiodentisticoguadagno@gmail.com
www.studiofrancescoguadagno.it

# AUTHORIZED DISTRIBUTORS OF CLARK PRODUCTS

## 1. UNITED STATES AND REST OF THE WORLD
Dr. Clark Research Association
8133 Engineer Rd
San Diego, CA 92111 – USA
P +1-800-220 3741
F +1-866-662 0086
customerservice@drclark.com
www.drclark.com

## 2. UNITED STATES
Superior Health Products
John Zumbo
13808 Ventura Boulevard
91423 Sherman Oaks, CA – USA
P +1-818-986 9456
F +1-818-986 8403
john@superiorhealthproducts.com
www.superiorhealthproducts.com

## 3. UNITED STATES
Tools for Healing LLC
5959 Shallowford Rd #221
Chattanooga, TN 37421 – USA
P +1-888-257 4273
F +1-423-648 7573
info@toolsforhealing.com
www.toolsforhealing.com

## 4. LATIN AMERICA
Dr. Mauricio Ulloa
19 avenida norte 1718 col. Layco
40604 San Salvador – El Salvador
P +503-222-69 065
climebio@gmail.com

# AUTHORIZED DISTRIBUTORS OF CLARK PRODUCTS

5. **MALAYSIA**
   CTA Wellness Center
   Steve Yap
   B.07/04 Blk B
   5th Fl, Gdn City Biz Ctr
   68000 Jln Dagang Besar, Tmn Dagang – Malaysia
   P +60-342-701 266
   F +60-342-701 831
   steve@ctawellness.com
   www.ctawellness.com

6. **RUSSIA AND BULGARIA**
   Dr. Clark Research Center
   Svetlana Manenkova
   Nijenburg 140
   1081GG Amsterdam – The Netherlands
   P +31-652-068 663
   info@doctor-clark.com
   www.doctor-clark.com

7. **UNITED KINGDOM**
   The Natural Health Choice Ltd
   Liam Young
   Logistics House, Charles Avenue
   RH15 9TQ Burgess Hill – UK
   P +44-1444-318 822
   F +44-845-018 1081
   info@the-natural-choice.co.uk
   www.the-natural-choice.co.uk

8. **GERMANY, SWITZERLAND AND REST OF EUROPE**
   Dr. Clark Zentrum
   Zieglerstrasse 44
   3007 Bern – Switzerland
   P +41-31-868 3131
   F +41-31-868 3132
   kundenservice@drclark.com
   www.drclark.com

# AUTHORIZED DISTRIBUTORS OF CLARK PRODUCTS

**9. THE NETHERLANDS**
Clark Nederland
Achterschouffert 67
6471VB Eygelshoven – The Netherlands
P +31-631-316 026
F +31-455-418 006
info@clarknederland.nl
www.clarknederland.nl

**10. SPAIN**
Nature & Clark
c/ Hortaleza, 106
28004 Madrid – Spain
Tel.: +34-91-594 2940
Fax: +34-91-445 9753
clientes@drclark.es
www.drclark.es

**11. FRANCE**
Vivre Naturellement SA
Covenant Bourdeles
22450 Hengoat – France
P +33-(0)3-91 83 27 90
vivrenaturel@gmail.com
www.vivrenaturellement.com

**12. ITALY**
Dr. Clark Service di Cosati Marina
CP 538
6903 Lugano – Switzerland (service for Italy)
P +41-76-495 3239
info@drclark.it
www.drclark.it

# AUTHORIZED DISTRIBUTORS OF CLARK PRODUCTS

### 13. ROMANIA
AS Ekilibrium SRL
Samoil isopescu 21
720036 Suceava – Romania
P +40-740-195 951
contact@ekilibrium.ro
www.ekilibrium.ro

### 14. FINLAND
Harjunhovi Oy
Lootuskauppa
02860 Espoo – Finland
P +358-50-585 4042
clientes@drclark.es
www.drclark.es